ESSENTIAL PSYCHOLOGY

**General Editor
Peter Herriot**

E3

THE PSYCHOLOGY OF TRAINING

ESSENTIAL

A

B

C

D

E

F

PSYCHOLOGY

THE
PSYCHOLOGY
OF TRAINING

**Robert Stammers and
John Patrick**

Methuen

First published in 1975 by Methuen & Co Ltd
11 New Fetter Lane, London EC4P 4EE
© *1975 Robert Stammers and John Patrick*
Printed in Great Britain by
Richard Clay (The Chaucer Press), Ltd
Bungay, Suffolk

ISBN (hardback) 0 416 83170 2
ISBN (paperback) 0 416 83180 X

We are grateful to Grant McIntyre of Open Books Publishing Ltd
for assistance in the preparation of this series.

Contents

Acknowledgements

The authors and publishers would like to thank the following for permission to reproduce some diagrams and tables in the text (for full bibliographic details please see References and Name Index):

The National Institute of Adult Education and the author for Fig. 1.2 reprinted from J. Annett (1968); A. T. Welford for Fig. 2.3 reprinted from A. T. Welford (1968); Taylor and Francis Ltd and the author for Fig. 2.4 reprinted from E. R. F. W. Crossman (1959); Holt, Rinehart and Winston for Figs 2.5 and 2.6 reprinted from G. A. Miller *et al* (1960), and Fig. 5.3 reprinted from R. M. Gagné (1970); the Controller of HMSO for Fig. 3.4 reprinted from J. Annett *et al* (1971); the Controller of HMSO for Figs 5.1 and 5.2 reprinted from M. Kay *et al* (1963); J. Hartley for Tables 5.1 and 5.2 reprinted from J. Hartley (1972a); Charles E. Merrill Publishing Co. for Figs 7.1 and 7.2 reprinted from E. A. Fleishman and W. E. Hempel Jr. (1955) and E. A. Fleishman and S. Rich (1963) respectively; Academic Press and the author for Fig. 7.3 reprinted from Talland (1968); the Controller of HMSO for Table 7.1 reprinted from D. B. Newsham (1969); Penguin and the author for Fig. 8.1 reprinted from M. Argyle (1967); and the Controller of HMSO for Fig. 8.3 and Table 8.1 reprinted from B. N. Lewis *et al* (1967).

I
Introduction

Overview

The study of training as an area of applied psychology poses a number of challenges. The first is one of definitions. What do we mean by training? Who are the trainees? Who are the trainers? What is the psychology of training? How and where do psychologists contribute to the training field? Whilst our main concern in this book is to answer the last question we shall briefly consider the question of definitions in this chapter, and also attempt to show the overlap of training with other related areas in applied psychology. Finally, in this chapter we will outline a popular view of training in a systems context, i.e. to view it as a component of man-machine system design, and to show how the various components of the training process themselves are interrelated.

In subsequent chapters this theme will be amplified. In Chapter 2, a basic model of man, the learner and the skilled performer, is presented. This should serve as a useful conceptual framework for subsequent ideas and innovations. Examination of tasks people are to be trained to perform represents a central topic in training and Chapter 3 outlines a number of approaches to task analysis. Training methods and equipment are other major areas and are covered by Chapters 4, 5 and 6. Firstly, Chapter 4 is concerned with the elimination and prevention of errors by the use of extrinsic feedback or guidance techniques. Chapter 5 explores the structuring and sequencing of material to be learned and Chapter 6 discusses simulators and other training equipment. Training adopts a normative approach by organizing the general conditions necessary for learning which enable trainees to perform the same task to the same criterion. But psychology, as we know, has shown us that people are different! Therefore the design of training must accommodate individual differences. Problems raised by this dilemma are discussed in Chapter 7. In the last chapter we discuss evaluation and try to point the way for training in the future. Emphasis is laid on the need for the training specialist to be able to cope with the demands of technological change. The importance of models and techniques which have generality and are not restricted to narrow areas of behaviour is also stressed. Now let us return to our definitions.

What is training?

Definitions, in the context of psychology, are always dangerous things. Most textbooks on training avoid this issue by simply embarking without definition, assuming their readers know what it is they are talking about. We cannot make such an assumption with this volume, addressed as it is to a wide readership. It is true to say that despite the efforts of training specialists, training practitioners and Government bodies, a variety of terminology exists. The Department of Employment's *Glossary of Training Terms* (1971) does however serve as a useful guide for the following:

Training:
The systematic development of the attitude/knowledge/skill behaviour pattern required by an individual in order to perform adequately a given task or job. This is often integrated or associated with further education. The use of learning experience to integrate the concept of training and education is increasingly common. cf. education.

Attitude/knowledge/skill behaviour pattern:
The essential determinants of effective performance in terms of attitude, knowledge and skill – the attitude to perform, the knowledge required to take the right attitude and the skills necessary to do it.

10

Skill:
An organized and co-ordinated pattern of mental and/or physical activity in relation to an object or other display of information, usually involving both receptor and effector processes. It is built up gradually in the course of repeated training or other experience. It is serial, each part from second to second is dependent on the last and influences the next. Skills may be described as perceptual-motor,* manual, intellectual, social, etc., according to the context or the most important aspect of the skill pattern.

Job:
All the tasks carried out by a particular person in the completion of his prescribed duties. In a wider context the term also covers the social and physical environment in which it is carried out.

Task:
A major element of work or a combination of elements of work by means of which a specific result is achieved.

Education:
Activities which aim at developing the knowledge, moral values, and understanding required in all walks of life rather than knowledge and skill relating to only a limited field of activity. The purpose of education is to provide the conditions essential for young persons and adults to develop an understanding of the traditions and ideas influencing the society in which they live, of their own and other cultures and of the laws of nature, and to acquire linguistic and other skills which are basic to learning, personal development, creativity and communication.

---

* Perceptual-motor skills involve the performance of tasks in the external world and are contrasted with verbal/language skills which manipulate signs and symbols representing the external world (Fitts and Posner, 1967); Holding (1965) suggests perceptual-motor tasks vary along a continuum in terms of 'perceptual' and 'motor' content. Tasks are classified as 'perceptual' when the stimulus elements of the task are dominant and as 'motor' when the execution of some bodily movement is paramount. The terms are therefore used as descriptive labels referring to different task situations and do not refer to mutually exclusive psychological phenomena. For example the execution of a simple (motor) hand movement necessarily depends on adequate proprioception (see Chapter 2) and maybe visual and auditory perception.

In essence, training is concerned with people learning to perform tasks, in the main, fairly specific and prescribed tasks, although there are exceptions where tasks are more open ended, e.g. in management and supervision. But, in general, learning in the training context is directed towards specific objectives whereas in education the objectives are more general and varied. Nevertheless academically it is impossible to always make clear distinctions. It quickly should be added that any particular learning exercise should have its objectives fairly carefully defined, whether it forms part of a 'training' or 'educational' programme. A compromise solution is to talk of 'instruction', which concentrates on the activity of preparing exercises with clear behavioural objectives, that is a clear statement of the performance requirements to be achieved by training (Mager, 1961). Differences then emerge between education and training more in the context of instructional activity than the actual methods used and objectives sought.

Glaser (1962) in a very useful review points out that a distinction is commonly made on the basis of two criteria: (a) the degree of specificity of objectives, and (b) on minimizing vs. maximizing individual differences. Training has more specific objectives, and attempts to minimize individual differences. He concludes: –

> One resolution of the training-education distinction is the following. Training and education are two aspects of the teaching process. The two terms refer to two classes of teaching processes that are not mutually exclusive. Certain dimensions which form the continuum along which the distinctions fall are specificity of behavioural goal, and uniformity vs. individual development. Although one may wish to distinguish between 'training' and 'education' in terms of behavioural goals and the methods of attaining them, the technological practices required to carry out either are built upon principles for modifying, developing and guiding behaviour that are generated from behavioural research. In the various definitions of the two verbs 'to train' and 'to educate', the underlying similarity is 'to develop or form by systematic instruction.' The term 'instruction' seems to be a word which can refer to the general operations with which both training and education are concerned. (1962:5.)

Contexts of training

The first and most important context is the occupational one in which people are learning certain jobs, or tasks within jobs. The young trainee or 'learner' obviously springs to mind. However, we must not neglect the training of people who change their jobs and also the training associated with changes in machinery and/or procedures. Training in industry is often a continuous ongoing activity at many different levels. There is operative training which is concerned with shop floor workers, apprenticeship schemes for 'skilled' jobs and clerical and management training.

It is important not to take too narrow a view of 'industry'. We are not just concerned with manufacturing industry. As well as producing goods, people are involved in distributing and selling them. We have large 'service' industries, e.g. hotel and catering and travel. Of course some occupations lie outside industry, providing various services to the community, e.g. local government and medical services. Thus occupational training concerns most people at some time or another. Military training, even outside of major conflict situations, is practically a full time activity of the armed services. Many innovations in both equipment and research have come from this area, some of which we will mention in later chapters.

A final area to consider is one that overlaps both occupational and recreational pursuits, that of sports or games. A number of us undertake instruction or coaching in order to learn new skills in the sports context. Here again the psychology of training is particularly relevant and there has been a useful cross-fertilization of ideas between psychologists and those concerned with sport skills. In the latter context we are concerned with people performing physical tasks i.e. perceptual-motor skills of one kind or another. In many job contexts such skilled performance is important. In view of this, and the large concentration of research work on perceptual-motor tasks, we have tended to adopt the view of man as an information processor (see A1 of *Essential Psychology*). It is important to remember however that many jobs do not involve perceptual-motor performance of the classic kind even though information processing may be important. Automation has led to many tasks which previously had relied on motor skill being replaced by those utilizing 'mental' skill (Crossman, 1960). Similarly in many service industries (e.g. airlines and retail distribution) where the work interface is person to person, social skills are important. In the next chapter we shall outline a simple model which goes some way to encompassing different types of work performance. Despite the generality of this approach it is nevertheless true to say that in the past, research by psychologists has concentrated on perceptual-motor skills – happily the picture is changing.

Training occurs in many contexts. There is, therefore, a wide range of people undergoing training. Concomitantly there will be a spread of expertise of people called trainers from professional trainers and coaches in some areas, to supervisors and key operatives in others. Just as people vary in their abilities to learn, they will also differ in their abilities to train others. Thus the psychologist's role emerges as one of improving the communication process that is training.

Training and the psychologist

Why should a psychologist be interested in training? The obvious answer to this is that training is about 'people learning' and that 'people learning' is a topic central to psychology. Training thus represents a view of the applied psychology of learning. As such one would expect to see the application to real life learning problems of principles established in the laboratory (see A3). To a limited extent this is true, but it is also true that many laboratory established principles have not held up when applied to real training problems (Gagné, 1962a). What is found is a cross current of laboratory and field results, gradually building up into a body of knowledge, emerging as a technology of training, e.g. Wallis (1966). Whilst some argue that laboratory research has its limitations, others see it as being a necessary, if long-term, approach. A middle course really is necessary. Learning itself is a complex affair. When carrying out experiments, therefore, the rigour of laboratory control is necessary. On the other hand results need to have relevance to practical problems. Therefore one looks for learning in tasks that are either real ones or which abstract their essential features. Follow-up studies in conjunction with the application of results in the field are also necessary. Unfortunately this is often missing.

The above discussion indicates that the psychologist is involved in training research, in its application, and also in the actual training programme. However, in the latter capacity he is more likely to be training a 'trainer' in, say, a new technique, rather than a 'trainee' in a particular task.

Let us now look at a typical research problem. A company training officer approaches the researcher with a fairly straightforward problem. Can he, by making an instructional film of a certain process, reduce the training time required for a job? The researcher will need to look at the tasks involved and consult the scientific literature on instructional films. He may be able to give some indication as to the potential value of a film in this context. It may emerge that there is insufficient research evidence and that some experimental work must be undertaken to provide the answer. An experiment can then be designed, with the normal methodological safeguards (see A8), to investigate the value of using such a film. This, somewhat idealized example illustrates how the role of training research may differ for the practitioner and the trainer. There is of course no reason why the latter should not be a psychologist as well. In this book we are not aiming at producing training researchers, or better trainers directly, but attempting to paint a picture of training as an area of applied psychology and to outline some of the main areas of research. Hopefully this should also indicate where psychologists could usefully direct their activities in the future.

Training and related areas

The overlap between training and education has already been discussed above and will not be pursued further here. Instead let us concentrate on the occupational context of training. If any task poses a problem to the performer, then we have three potential solutions:

1 Select people who through their aptitudes, abilities or previous training can deal with the particular task demands.
2 Train people to deal with these demands.
3 Design, or redesign, the job situation in order to reduce the task demands.

Each of these solutions will meet the required objectives, although by different routes and with different specialisms of applied psychology. The first is concerned with personnel selection, and the third with ergonomics or man-machine system design. Although this book is primarily concerned with training, it is important to remember that such a range of alternatives exist in the real world situation. It is of course possible to use more than one approach, or in fact all three. But the extent to which any of them will be used will depend upon a number of factors, many of which lie outside the control of the applied psychologist:

(a) available financial resources
(b) available labour
(c) traditions or established precedents
(d) current fashions in the human resources field
(e) availability of specialist advice
(f) time constraints
(g) expected life of process

In the last section of this chapter, training will again be examined as a system that necessarily interacts with other systems.

Therefore to isolate the area of training, as is necessary, makes certain assumptions. Firstly that some form of selection of trainees has already occurred, and that data on their abilities and previous learning is available. To use the jargon term, it is impossible to devise a training programme without knowing the 'target population'. Such information is needed to decide upon how detailed the training need be and at what pace it should proceed. Trainees with previous experience of a similar task will require different training from those newly recruited. Intelligence is an important variable determining style and pace of instruction. It can be seen therefore that there is a close relationship between personnel selection and training. If there is a labour shortage and less able people are selected then more training will have to be given. If there is a large labour pool, the best qualified can be selected and they may require little training. Selection criteria influence the training system designer's work, as does the design of the man-machine system for which training is being devised.

It is to be assumed that, ideally, people will not be trained to operate a badly designed system. Unfortunately this ideal is not always met, and sometimes a man may have to be trained to get information from a badly designed display where a better display would eliminate the need for training. A system may be designed with an inherent lag between a control movement and its displayed effect. Such systems are difficult to control and an improved display control relationship can make the task less difficult to learn. There is a close relationship between training and ergonomics. Men can be trained to control badly designed systems but is this the best solution? What happens in an emergency, or when the man is fatigued or otherwise stressed? It is surely far better to reduce as far as possible the chance of error, fatigue and discomfort by the use of ergonomics. However, there is a dilemma. Such an approach would design the man out of the system completely taken to its logical extreme. This certainly would reduce training problems but it is not only sometimes impractical but also undesirable because of job satisfaction decreasing with monotonous tasks. A far better approach is one that looks at an optimal man-machine system design which makes use of the superior features of both man and machine. This is the emerging view in applied psychology, thus maintaining the skills and dignity of men in the design of systems – a viewpoint if not yet a reality.

Finally the use of job aids also overlaps both the areas of training and system design. These are written or pictorial aids that assist people at work. Rather than memorizing a long list of instructions for starting the process, the man can be given a list. An algorithm or decision tree can aid someone in locating a fault (Lewis *et al*, 1967). The use of such aids obviously affects the kind and amount of training that is given. This area will be further explored in Chapter 3. Training therefore interacts and overlaps with other areas of applied psychology. As such it is useful to look at training as a system and its interactions with other systems.

A systems approach to training

A systems approach is one which basically looks at the different functions of the components of any process and examines their interrelations not only with each other but with other processes. It is extremely important to determine the nature of these interactions as well as the nature of the components themselves. This is because one aim of the systems approach is to predict the nature and direction of change in the remaining components by a change in one or more of the others. As such this approach can view any functioning entity as a system, the important thing being to define its objectives. In other words a system is defined in terms of what it is attempting to achieve. Thus we can view a car, a school, a factory, a shop, etc. as a system, and analyse their objectives and how they set out to achieve them.

One can view systems hierarchically. A man in his working environment can be analysed as a man-machine system but this system is also a part of the overall production line of the factory. Such a hierarchical approach can be extended upwards, to view the factory as part of a company, which is itself a part of an industrial system, or downwards where man consists of a number of subsystems, e.g. perception, memory, etc. Therefore as well as considering the interactions between components in the system we must consider also the interactions between systems. Such interactions may be between systems on the same level or at higher or lower levels of the hierarchy. An 'interaction' between systems or components of systems refers to a transfer of energy, objects, control or information. Such forms of transfer may be in one or both directions. In the latter case transfer may involve feedback from one component to another, thus enabling it to become self-regulating. Consider the training system that transfers too many trainees to the factory floor. This will cause a transfer of information back to the manager of the training system to reduce his output. This in turn should cause a change in the role of the 'recruitment and selection of trainees' component, reducing its intake. The systems approach therefore offers a basically simple philosophy for looking at the way things work and interact with each other. Its attraction lies in its generality and potential for successfully predicting changes in the system from changes in the components. Such predictions can be more or less exact depending on the degree of reliability of the rules governing interactions between components of the system(s).

We have already introduced a systems view of training by mentioning the interactions between training, selection and ergonomics. The training system objectives could be altered depending on the selection criteria and the man-machine system design. There are therefore influences outside of the training function that affect how it can work. Before examining this, let us firstly explore what are the components of the training system and how they interrelate.

There are various systems views of training, many of which have been derived from a military context. A representative one by Eckstrand (1964) is shown in Fig. 1.1 where the system is analysed into its various components. Firstly the objectives of this particular training programme must be defined (1).

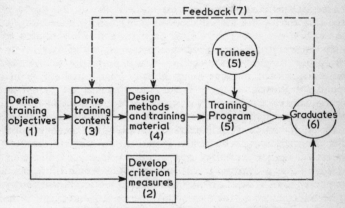

Fig. 1.1 *Eckstrand's (1964) training system*

From this it is then possible to develop criterion tests (2) i.e. measures which will indicate whether people have obtained these objectives, after training. An interesting point here is that, ideally, if the people 'fail' such tests then it is not they that have failed but the system. A third stage is to specify what should go into training in order for those objectives to be met (3). The next stage involves actually devising training methods and equipment in order to present information to the trainees (4). The trainees and material come together in the training programme (5), and the trainees emerge as graduates of this programme (6) (not necessarily, of course, as university graduates). They are then measured against the criterion measures, any discrepancies causing modifications to be made to appropriate components by virtue of the feedback loops (7). For example, if one test item was repeatedly failed then a new method of presenting it (modification of 4) may be needed. Alternatively, not enough information may be presented and the training content may need changing (modification of 3). Such a flow diagram is characteristic of the systems approach, helping us to represent the process at work and how parts interact.

This book will examine the contribution of psychology to this process, concentrating on the components in isolation. It is well to remember their interrelations however. It is also important to remember the fact that the training function is in turn part of a larger system, the organization. The applied psychologist has constraints on him other than the limitation of the boundaries of knowledge on his subject. Anyone working in the real world soon comes up against the difficulties caused by external events. A very good training programme may be devised but prove to be too costly, or an imperfect simulator may have to be used because it has already been purchased. Such examples illustrate the need for full specification of system components according to the practical contingencies of the real world, rather than an ideal or academic viewpoint. The answer may be of course to demonstrate that although the new training programme may be costly, it will in the long run be cost-effective, i.e. pay for itself and more, by increased efficiency.

Fig. 1.2 is a diagram from Annett (1968) which illustrates a wider systems view of training than that mentioned previously. The basic inputs to the system are manpower and physical resources. These determine both the nature of the trainees and the trainers, what the task will be like, where the training goes on and what material can be used for training. These, in turn, give rise to 'regulators' of the system, ranging from attitudes to choice of materials used. A training situation is then designed, which can be measured in various ways. The most obvious way is of course production, but other more subtle measures are possible and sometimes very necessary, especially where tasks are not directly productive, e.g. labour turnover. Finally the system must be evaluated, and hopefully an index of cost-effectiveness could be derived. Feedback from this to the design, regulators or financial resources components should make the training and ultimately the overall system more efficient. It appears therefore that the training specialist should beware of becoming too much of a specialist. He should not forget the context of his work. Nevertheless he still needs his specialist skills and in the rest of the book we look at the contribution of psychology to them.

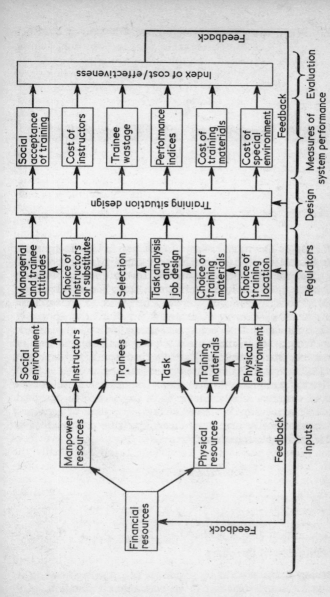

Fig. 1.2 *Outline of the training system (Annett, 1968)*

2
The human skill model

In this chapter the contribution of skill psychology to training will be examined. If it is possible to erect a general model of skilled performance then suggestions for facilitating learning should emerge. Psychological principles from classical learning theories are briefly reviewed and their relevance to understanding the process of learning is discussed. An alternative approach derived from studies of perceptual-motor skill is developed. Benefits from work in these areas are due to the application of a new conceptual framework rather than specific theoretical ideas. The model of man as an information processor is applied to the learning of tasks and is shown to be generally useful outside of the narrow area of motor skills from which it was derived. Skill acquisition is viewed as the integration of activities into a hierarchically organized structure. The utility of such ideas for training is mentioned.

Classical learning theory

Learning is one of the most controversial and intensively studied topics in psychology (see A3). Hill (1972) provides a useful summary whilst Hilgard and Bower (1966) give a thorough review. There is little disagreement over the operational definition of learning:

Learning is the process by which an activity originates or is changed through reacting to an encountered situation, provided that the characteristics of the change in activity cannot be explained on the basis of native response tendencies, maturation or temporary states of the organism (e.g. fatigue and drugs, etc.). (Hilgard and Bower, 1966:2)

Learning is therefore a hypothetical state which can only be inferred from the observation of measurable performance. This distinction between learning and performance is important and often neglected. Changes in the level of learning may not be reflected in changes in behaviour. The student who has mastered some new concepts must be given the appropriate *opportunity* to manifest evidence of this new learning. On the other hand changes in performance will not necessarily be due to changes in level of learning, as the student suffering from severe examination nerves will attempt to convince his teacher.

There are many different and conflicting theoretical approaches to learning. It is useful to classify them in terms of the nature of the fundamental concepts used to represent learning and the conditions which are deemed necessary for learning to occur (Spence, 1951). In terms of the concepts used to represent learning the *cognitive* concepts of Köhler, Koffka, Lewin and Tolman may be contrasted with the *stimulus-response* elements adopted by Thorndike, Hull, Guthrie and Skinner. In the second division, the principle of *contiguity* (i.e. association) proposed by Guthrie, Tolman and Lewin is very different to that of *reinforcement* advocated by Thorndike, Hull and Skinner. Undoubtedly the conceptualization of learning as the reinforcement of stimulus-response connections has been the most influential approach. This was due to the analysis of behaviour in terms of reflexes at the beginning of the century, coupled with a preoccupation with animal experimentation and a growing insistence that psychology should reject armchair philosophy and become the science of human behaviour. However, psychologists have become increasingly disillusioned with a straightforward stimulus-response reinforcement paradigm.

Application of the principle of reinforcement has been seen as a panacea in many areas concerned with learning difficulties (e.g. education). The origins of reinforcement theory began with the publication of *Animal Intelligence* by E. L. Thorndike in 1898 who observed the consistent behaviour of cats escaping from puzzle boxes. Learning was seen as the gradual strengthening of connections between a stimulus (S) and a response (R).

Such strengthening was principally governed by the *Law of Effect* according to Thorndike. When an S-R connection was followed by a satisfying state of affairs, the strength of that connection was increased. Thorndike in 1913 defined a satisfying state of affairs as 'one which the animal does nothing to avoid, often doing things which maintain or renew it'.

Conversely an annoying state of affairs would weaken the strength of an S-R connection. After 1930 however, Hilgard and Bower (1966) pointed out that Thorndike had relegated the latter complementary aspect of effect theory. It is impossible to detail here the manifold developments of reinforcement theory (see Kimble, 1961). Suffice it to say that C. L. Hull in his book *Principles of Behaviour* (1943) linked the principle of reinforcement with a reduction in biological drives. Probably the most influential writer in this area has been B. F. Skinner (1953). He has adopted an atheoretical position stressing the role of reinforcement in operant conditioning as the basis for controlling behaviour. The important aspect of the reinforcement position is that it maintains that S-R learning occurs *automatically* after the occurrence of a desirable reinforcer contingent upon the correct response. In human learning the words 'right' and 'good' are reinforcers commonly used. Learning is therefore conceived as the increase of some responses which are rewarded.

Reinforcement theories are burdened with philosophical and logical objections and are contradicted by some specific experimental findings (Postman, 1947). Furthermore they neglect the dynamic, interacting and adaptive complexity of human learning situations. They fail to emphasize that the learner requires *information* in order to be able to learn a task. It may be that the informational value of reinforcers such as 'good' or 'right' is the determinant of learning rather than their motivational value. The essential information may be provided by a number of different methods (see Ch. 4) which do not necessarily involve information provided after execution of a response. It will be shown that such methods may be equivalent or sometimes superior at promoting learning.

Cybernetics and information theory

Limitations of the human operator were found with the wartime development of new weapon and radar systems. For the first time, psychologists working with engineers and physiologists tackled the problems of efficient equipment design in order to maximize both speed and accuracy of human performance (Fitts, 1951). There was clearly a need for a general theoretical framework which could be used to describe, measure and predict performance of very different tasks. Two important publications just after the war profoundly influenced psychologists' ideas about human performance. In 1948 Wiener's *Cybernetics* conceptualised man as a self-governing system both in physiological and psychological terms and *The Mathematical Theory of Communication* of Shannon (1948) set out the basic concepts of information, sometimes called communication theory.

One fundamental principle of the cybernetic approach was that of *feedback control* derived from communication engineer-

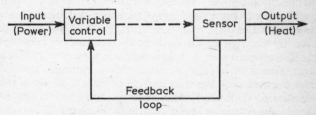

Fig. 2.1 *Feedback control by a thermostat*

ing systems. Feedback control simply means that the output of any system may regulate or control the input to the system. A simple example of such a system is a thermostat (see Fig. 2.1). The temperature is regulated because information from the 'sensor', by affecting the 'variable control', determines the level of power input to the system. If the temperature increases above the specified level then the input of power will be reduced until the desired temperature is attained. Similarly a drop in temperature will produce a subsequent increase in power to the system. The system is therefore self-regulating. Such regulation is only possible because of the feedback loop and such a system is therefore considered to be closed-loop and under feedback control. Without such a feedback loop the system will be 'open-loop' and unable to adapt to environmental demands, e.g. a traditional coal fire. However a person may constitute the feedback loop. Indeed both machine and man-machine systems will function poorly if the feedback loop is inappropriately designed. For

25

example, imagine that you are taking a shower. The problem is to select the correct position of the temperature control as quickly as possible using one's body as a 'sensor' of the temperature of the water. In other words one must translate any discrepancy of actual and intended temperature into the right control displacement. The discovery of this appropriate 'transformation rule' (Annett, 1969), as some may have experienced, is often painfully difficult. It is also worth mentioning that in this example the efficiency of such feedback control will also be a function of the speed with which 'information' can be processed both by the human and machine elements of the system. One time lag will occur between movement of the shower control and a change in the temperature of the water. A second lag will occur between the recipient's perception of the temperature and translation into any necessary action. The longer the duration of either of these time delays the more difficult the system will be to control.

The introduction of the concept of information from communication engineering complemented the principle of feedback control. Shannon (1948) developed various mathematical theorems concerned with the transmission of signals. Some of these theorems and their application in psychology have been well discussed by Attneave (1959) although a useful introductory summary is to be found in Fitts and Posner (1967). The importance of this approach has been to provide a general framework in which to compare diverse aspects of human performance.

Let us first introduce some of the main concepts from communication theory relevant to our general model of the skill learner. Firstly a signal contains *information*, the amount of which is defined by the degree of uncertainty which it eliminates. Such uncertainty can be manipulated in three ways: – a) by altering the number of possible signals which may occur, b) by altering the probability associated with the occurrence of any one or more, c) by introducing sequential dependencies between two or more signals (Edwards, 1964). Thus taking the most simple situation (a), the amount of information available in a signal increases as the number of possible alternatives increase. Therefore a letter of the alphabet contains more information than a single digit (assuming that the alternatives are equiprobable) because it resolves more uncertainty. Quantitative measures of the amount of information can be made which are independent of the *nature* of the task thus making intertask

26

comparisons possible. Another important aspect of information theory is that the signal is transmitted along what is termed a *communication channel*. In Shannon's terms such a channel may take many physical forms, e.g. a cable or the atmosphere. Crossman (1964) represents the characteristics of any communication channel (Fig 2.2). The signal to be sent must be 'encoded' with reference to a 'code-book' which provides the translation rules enabling it to be transmitted along the channel. Likewise it must be 'decoded' before it can be received. However transmission along the communication channel is unlikely to be free from 'noise'. The word noise is used in a technical sense not only

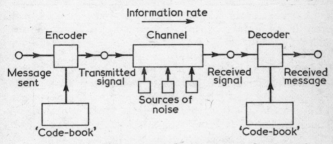

Fig. 2.2 *Characteristics of an information channel (Crossman, 1964)*

referring to interference in the auditory modality but to any perturbation which produces distortion of the signal and therefore increases the likelihood of error in reception. Shannon also states that there will exist some *limit* to the *capacity* of any particular channel. This implies that there will be a maximum possible rate of transmission of information along that channel. Another important concept related to that of 'noise' is *redundancy*. Signals are redundant if they contain less than the maximal amount of information and may therefore be used if the communication channel is perturbed by a lot of 'noise'. For example, 'the English language is redundant for two reasons. First the probability of occurrence is not equal for all letters, E, for example, is much more likely to occur than Q. Second, the probability of a letter's occurring is greatly affected by the letters which occurred previously.' (Fitts and Posner 1967: 91) Such redundant underlying features of language are useful for recognising a word which is poorly typed or spoken.

The most influential approach to the study of skilled performance has been to regard the human operator as an information processing channel (e.g. Welford, 1968). Fig 2.3 presents such a system from Welford. Such block diagrams are derived from the communication channel model and integrate both the concept of *information* and *feedback control*.

This can be regarded as a general model of skilled performance which has implications for the training of any task. The

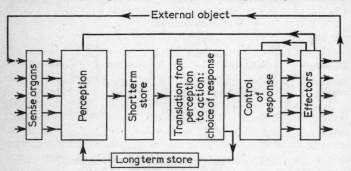

Fig. 2.3 *Hypothetical block diagram of the human sensori-motor system. Only a few of the many feedback-loops which exist are shown (Welford, 1968)*

essential elements of performance of any task can be characterized as a sequence of input, action and feedback. However, it is true to say that application of such a model has occurred principally with perceptual-motor tasks (see A5). One disadvantage of the general approach is that it assumes that there is a sufficient amount of 'energy' (Edwards, 1964) to enable information to be transmitted. In other words it assumes that imperfect performance is due to limitations of information transmission rather than the performer being fatigued, etc. A fuller description of human performance would include consideration of such 'activation' levels of the operator.

Input to action

Firstly the *input* information is received by the operator via his sense organs. These may be divided into *interoceptors* which initiate sensations of pain, hunger and thirst, *exteroceptors* which sense the immediate external environment (i.e. touch and warmth), *distance* receptors (eyes, ears and nose) and *proprioceptors*. At this juncture it is worth recognizing that there is considerable confusion between the terms 'proprioception' and 'kinaesthesis'. Proprioception here is taken as the more global concept which embraces both the 'kinaesthetic' sensations of movement (Adams, 1968), discrimination of limb and body location and the sense of balance provided by the inner ear. Proprioception is therefore not a unitary sense but is a super-ordinate concept under which are subsumed many different aspects of bodily perception. A correlational study by Scott (1955), who examined a battery of twenty-eight tests of proprioception (ranging from balancing to arm positioning), confirms that different aspects of proprioceptive ability are independent of each other. Later in this chapter the importance of proprioception as feedback in skilled performance will be examined in greater detail.

There is a great deal of information continuously impinging on the human's sense organs but only some of this is available for 'translation from perception to action' (see Fig. 2.3). Information is filtered, recognized, integrated, stored and sometimes lost as it passes through the 'perception' and 'short-term' memory parts of the human sensori-motor system. The characteristics of these processes are more thoroughly presented in Welford (1968).

The information from the receptor processes must be interpreted, organized and eventually translated into a course of action which may, if necessary, result in responses which are executed by the effectors. Any information to be processed may be categorized as to whether or not it arises as a consequence of the learner's actions. If it does it is termed feedback. Otherwise it refers to cues which direct action, a special case of which is the task 'input'. In the latter sense the trainee should have some information on the task objectives *before* feedback can be used to adapt actions to those demanded by the task (see Ch. 4).

The ease of 'translation from perception to action' for any signals will depend partly upon their rate of occurrence and the amount of information they carry. Studies of human information processing, particularly studies of reaction time, have demonstrated the limited capacity of this part of the system. If the time interval between two successive signals is less than approximately 0.5 seconds, then the response to the second stimulus is delayed longer than a normal reaction time, indicating that processing of signals is successive rather than in parallel. This phenomenon has been termed the 'psychological refractory period' and can be largely accounted for by assuming that the operator behaves as a 'single channel'. Furthermore Hick (1952) found a constant rate of information transmission from reaction time studies in which speed of reaction increased linearly with a measure of the informational content of a signal. However, the concept of a fixed information processing capacity has been questioned in the light of studies involving practice, compatibility between input and output, and task variety, all of which have produced markedly different processing rates. The applicability of these informational concepts to skilled performance remains an area of controversy, particularly because of the flexible and adaptive manner in which capacity can be utilized (Moray, 1967).

The last stage of the information processing model before input is converted into action or output, is the effector process. After the receptor information has been translated into a proposed course of action, the latter must be executed by commands to the effector organs of the body (e.g. a movement of the hands or legs). Some of our knowledge of the organization of the effector system stems from analyses of simple hand movements. Fitts (1954) formulated a relationship between accuracy, amplitude, and time of movement in informational terms. He observed reciprocal tapping between two targets and discovered that if the ratio between amplitude of movement and width of the target remained constant, then the movement time was the same. The logarithm of this ratio was used to define 'the index of difficulty' of any movement in information theory terms. Movement time increased linearly with this index of difficulty, which is consistent with the notion that the rate of information transmission was constant. Fitts and Peterson (1964) found that this was also characteristic of a task involving discrete movements. Discrete perceptual-motor tasks are usually different to continuous ones in a number of ways. Discrete tasks tend to be self-paced with distinct response units such as manipulating a switch. Performance is reflected by the speed and/or number of errors. In contrast continuous tasks are typically paced with a continuously changing stimulus input, ideally requiring a continuous adjustive response. For example, when driving a car, technically described by psychologists as a tracking task, hopefully the driver follows or tracks the continuous road by appropriate manipulations of the wheel. In the laboratory measures of performance of such 'tracking' tasks would be integrated error or the amount of time in which the tracker maintained a response within certain limits of the target. However, as in other aspects of performance, the rate of information transmission in such tasks varies as a result of other factors, e.g. practice.

Feedback

In the information processing model of skill, feedback arises as a consequence of the learner's actions. The term feedback used here has alternatively been labelled knowledge of results (Annett, 1961), information feedback (Bilodeau, 1966) and, of course, reinforcement. Many writers have stressed the importance of feedback for both learning and performance, amongst the most prominent are Annett (1969) and Adams (1968). In this section different types of feedback will be distinguished and their contribution to the regulation of skilled performance discussed.

Intrinsic versus extrinsic feedback. A useful dichotomy can be made between intrinsic and extrinsic feedback (Annett, 1961) and should not be confused with that between internal and external feedback. Intrinsic feedback refers to that which is available to a person in the *normal* task situation and may therefore be transmitted via any modality. Extrinsic feedback refers to additional information which is not available in performance of the normal task. This type of feedback may be supplied by either man or machine or both. Consider the problem of learning to play squash. The player will normally receive relevant proprioceptive, visual and auditory feedback during the game, which is therefore labelled intrinsic. Nevertheless a coach may supply additional information in any modality concerning movement of the racket, general strategy, etc. and this is providing extrinsic feedback which will be absent after training. Some investigations which have demonstrated the importance of the relationship between intrinsic and extrinsic feedback and the optimal means of presenting extrinsic feedback for learning will be reviewed in Chapter 4.

Action versus learning feedback. A distinction is often drawn between *action* feedback which is available during execution of a

31

response and may be used to maintain performance, and *learning* feedback which occurs after a response and may therefore improve future responses (Miller, 1953). Both action and learning feedback are forms of extrinsic feedback since they will be removed after training. The classification is based firstly on whether feedback effects learning and secondly on the temporal relationship between feedback and response. The latter distinction coincides with that between terminal and concurrent feedback mentioned in Chapter 4. However, the former criterion can only be determined by empirical observation. It seems likely that action feedback was so named because in many experiments concurrent feedback was often only a prop to performance, and when removed revealed no learning had really taken place. Annett (1959) presents an experiment demonstrating this phenomenon, in which subjects were required to learn to apply a pressure. Comparison was made between a group provided with continuous visual (action) feedback by the movement of an indicator and another given feedback only after each attempt was completed. The former group were considerably inferior to the latter when feedback was removed after training. These findings therefore only emphasize that some types of extrinsic feedback which will be unavailable after training, may fail to be effective at promoting learning. The distinction is misleading because some types of feedback provided concurrent with the response can effect learning as will be shown in Chapter 4. Of course, this can only be ascertained 'necessarily *post hoc*' (Annett, 1961) when the extrinsic feedback loop has been removed. Therefore the distinction between action and learning feedback is unfortunately named and will not by reference to *when* feedback occurs necessarily predict its effectiveness for learning.

The importance of this distinction is in drawing attention to the fact that the trainee must learn the task during training in such a manner that removal of the extrinsic cues after training has no effect. There are a number of possible explanations of why removal of action feedback may produce a decrease in level of performance. The trainee may simply be unaware of the forthcoming change in task conditions after training which will delimit learning. Another explanation is that the visual action feedback in the above experiments distracts the trainee from learning the important intrinsic proprioceptive cues of the task. Annett (1970) on the other hand advances evidence favouring an intersensory explanation which suggests that learning is dependent upon the summation of visual and proprioceptive feedback, so that when one source is removed, learning will suffer. No matter which explanation is adopted, it is still empirically true that removal of visual concurrent feedback often leads to poor learning, particularly of simple perceptual-motor skills.

The importance of intrinsic feedback. Implicit in the information processing model of skill is the assumption that intrinsic feedback will be used to regulate ongoing action. Basically two research strategies have been employed to evaluate the importance of the different intrinsic feedback loops (particularly the visual, auditory, and proprioceptive loops). Such feedback loops may either be eliminated or manipulated in some manner and the subsequent effect on performance recorded. Two general problems are associated with such strategies. The usual degree of performance impairment may be masked by the greater utilization of other available feedback loops. For example blindfold subjects may be able to compensate for the loss of visual feedback by increased use of proprioceptive feedback. Furthermore the degree of impairment may be task specific.

Auditory and visual feedback loops are relatively easy to both eliminate and manipulate. Manipulations may involve either some distortion or delay of the feedback. Distortion of the nature of visual feedback has been accomplished by the wearing of special spectacles (Stratton, 1896) and the use of closed-circuit television (Smith, 1966). These studies show that whilst such transformations of feedback as inversion of the visual image are initially disruptive, considerable adaptation is possible after practice. The effect of delayed auditory and visual feedback can more permanently disturb skilled performance. Lee (1951) found that a brief delay in the auditory feedback from speech induced the speaker to reduce speed and even stutter. Similarly Smith (1966) reported that even practice with delayed visual feedback produced an insignificant improvement.

An essential element of any skilled performance is efficient movement control in both spatial and temporal dimensions. One possible basis for such control and regulation of ongoing performance is the intrinsic proprioceptive feedback which has previously been mentioned. The obvious difficulties associated with eliminating or manipulating such internal feedback has stimulated a number of ingenious attempts at evaluating the importance of proprioception. There are three different approaches to assessing the effect of eliminating proprioceptive feedback. 1) Laszlo (1967) attempted to eliminate proprioceptive feedback by means of a nerve compression block strapped to the upper arm. In a tapping task relearning occurred in the absence of proprioceptive feedback and learning was also possible with the total elimination of peripheral cues. These results clearly depend on the efficiency of Laszlo's technique which has recently been questioned. 2) A classic study by Lashley (1917) of a man with complete anaesthesia of the left knee as a result of a gun shot injury showed surprisingly, in the absence of any peripheral feedback, that the man was still able to control and repeat movements remarkably well although he was unable to compensate for changing conditions. These two sources both suggest that control of simple repetitive movements may occur at the same central level by selection of some 'motor programme' (Keele 1968) which can be executed independently of any intrinsic proprioceptive feedback. 3) Accurate 'ballistic' movements can be executed which are faster than the time required to process proprioceptive feedback. However it is necessary to redress any imbalance in case the reader is assuming that proprioceptive feedback is not essential to skilled performance. Such feedback is vital to efficient performance of particularly complex skills or adaption to changing conditions of simple skills. The clinical case of *tabes dorsalis* provides an example of the disruption caused by the absence of proprioceptive feedback. Movement control for the sufferer is impossible without visual feedback and even with it is inefficient (Wiener, 1948).

A different approach has manipulated the quality and/or quantity of proprioceptive feedback available in tracking tasks. This can be accomplished by changing the dynamics of the control stick used by the tracker, e.g. by additional spring loading. Gibbs (1954) found a pressure control superior to a freemoving control in a tracking task, which he attributed to superior proprioceptive feedback. Whilst this is intuitively appealing, Keele (1968) has isolated two weaknesses in this argument. Firstly a change in performance associated with a change in proprioceptive feedback conditions does not of course necessarily mean that movement is regulated by intrinsic proprioceptive feedback. In the above tracking example it could be argued that programming of movements for force is better than for distance. Secondly, a change in performance could be explained on the basis that the longer movement is more difficult to execute.

In conclusion, therefore, whilst many writers agree that proprioceptive feedback serves an important regulatory function in skilled performance a strict interpretation of many types of evidence is difficult because it is always logically possible for control to be based on some motor programme. There are other reasons for suspecting that proprioceptive feedback is important. Proprioceptive processing time appears to be shorter than the estimate of 190–260 milliseconds required for processing visual feedback (Keele and Posner, 1968). Therefore performance of tasks requiring fast and accurate movements may be ultimately better controlled by proprioceptive feedback. Such feedback may also provide the basis for accurately timing future activity (Adams and Creamer, 1962). Skilled activity is characterized by an ability to anticipate forthcoming events and therefore respond without the lag of a normal reaction time. The evidence shows that such anticipation improves when the person engages in a prior activity involving proprioceptive feedback. One possible explanation of this phenomenon is that the decaying characteristics of proprioceptive feedback associated with previous action will serve as a cue of when to initiate a future action, thus improving temporal accuracy.

Dynamics of skill acquisition

In the previous section a general information processing model of skill has been sketched with different hypothetical stages mediating input into action and many different feedback loops providing the trainee with information. It should be recognized that this is only a general model and the importance of these stages and the various feedback loops will be a product of a variety of factors. Firstly the nature of any particular task will determine the perceptual and short-term memory demands and the ease of translation from perception to action. In some highly habitual tasks, the conversion of input to action may be direct and automatic, using little or no channel capacity, with the effector process highly organized. Secondly the individual abilities of the learner will determine how well these task demands may be met and this topic will be examined in Chapter 7. Thirdly the stage or level of skill will affect the importance of both input to action processes and the different feedback loops.

Theories of skill acquisition. The contribution of four theories to our understanding of skill acquisition will be examined:—
1) the progression hypothesis, 2) Crossman's selection theory, 3) Adams' closed-loop theory of motor learning and 4) Fitts' hypothesised three stages.

1) In tracking tasks the human operator's output via a control stick can be related to the input or tracking error which is displayed. This relationship is termed the 'human transfer function'. It can be described in terms of the characteristics of the error signal utilized (i.e. its amplitude, velocity or acceleration). It was found that initially during training, control was based on the amplitude characteristics of the error signal and progressed to control based on the more subtle velocity and later acceleration components (Fuchs, 1962). This was called the *progression* hypothesis. A complementary notion was that the breakdown of skill under stress would see the *regression* of control to that based on the simplest characteristics of the error signal. As yet such a theory has not been applied in the area of training. Nevertheless, training may be facilitated by information emphasizing these aspects of the error signal.

2) Crossman (1959) proposes that skill acquisition is a process of the operator selecting the most appropriate method from his repertoire. Observing data collected from studies of repetitive manual skills where speed was at a premium, he was impressed with the decreased cycle time with practice. An example of the shift in the distribution of cycle times for a torch switch assembly task is presented in Fig. 2.4. The experienced worker performs faster than the trainee. According to Crossman, 'practice exerts a selective effect on the operator's behaviour, favouring those patterns of action which are quickest at the expense of others'.

The implication for training is that the trainer must ensure that the best methods are available for selection from the trainee's repertoire. This may be accomplished most effectively by 'guiding' the trainee through the correct patterns of action rather than relying on a trial and error procedure. Once the appropriate pattern is available, extrinsic feedback to the trainee may facilitate the acquisition of speed.

3) Adams considers as the basis of skill acquisition, the learning of graded movements. Learning proceeds through two stages, verbal-motor and then motor. Essential for learning and movement is the establishment of a 'perceptual trace' which 'is

36

the construct which fundamentally determines the extent of movement and it is what S [subject] uses as the reference to adjust his next movement on the basis of the KR [feedback] he has received' (Adams, 1971: 123). In the verbal-motor stage extrinsic feedback is particularly important in gradually developing a more accurate 'perceptual trace'. Verbal cues provide information in terms of general instructions concerning the task and feedback about previous movements. Such verbal information is critical in the first stage of learning but becomes

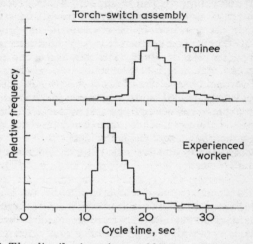

Fig. 2.4 *The distribution of assembly times for a trainee and an experienced worker (Crossman, 1959)*

redundant on transition to the second, motor, stage when the perceptual trace is well established. A recent investigation, using a discrete movement, by Boucher (1974) finds that a verbal task performed after extrinsic feedback associated with a movement is particularly detrimental in the early stages of acquisition. This is consistent with Adams' notion of an early verbal-motor stage. However, to account for the possibility of error even when the perceptual trace is well established, it is also necessary to postulate the existence of a 'memory trace whose role is to select and initiate the response, preceding the use of the perceptual trace' (Adams, 1971: 125).

This bears some resemblance to Crossman's theory, and maybe an increasing memory trace is involved with the selection of the more appropriate movement patterns during training. However, Adams is vague about how the memory trace is established and he only appears to consider it relevant to the selection of the movement *direction* which is usually predetermined in many laboratory experiments on discrete movements. If a number of movements are made in the same direction, one might ask how the appropriate perceptual trace is selected if the memory trace is only concerned with direction? A number of subsequent experiments held to support Adams' theory are only demonstrations of the previously acknowledged fact that feedback is critical to acquisition of simple skill.

4) Probably the most influential theory of skill acquisition was proposed by Fitts (1962). These ideas stemmed from his own experiments and the opinions of pilot trainers and sports coaches concerning various types of skill learning. Fitts postulates that the development of skilled performance passes through three phases: the cognitive, associative and autonomous. These stages may overlap and transition from one to the next tends to be a continuous rather than a sudden change. Therefore we can only certainly state that the first and third stages will not overlap. In the 'cognitive' phase:

> Students and instructors attempt to analyse tasks and to verbalise about what is being learned. What to expect and what to do is emphasised, procedures are described, and information is provided about errors which often are frequent. (Fitts, 1962: 187)

This stage certainly describes the acquisition of some complex tasks in which new rules and concepts must be understood before they can be efficiently executed. The person has to develop an overall plan. For example, the novice squash player has to learn the rules and strategies of the game in an initial 'intellectualization' process. Verbal pre-training has been shown to be useful even in tracking tasks. Generally tasks will vary in their comparative complexity and sometimes this component may be minimal. The problem is that Fitts' formulation does not allow us to predict in advance the degree of importance of any stage.

The 'associative' phase is characterized by the establishment of the correct patterns of behaviour by practice, with errors being gradually eliminated. The efficiency of different methods

38

of presenting and sequencing information to establish such 'associations' is discussed in Chapters 4, 5 and 6.

The final 'autonomous' stage of learning is similar to Adams' second 'motor' stage. Fitts states,

It is characterized by

(a) gradually increasing speed of performance in tasks where it is important to improve time or accuracy scores far beyond the point where errors, as ordinarily defined, can be detected, and

(b) gradually increasing resistance to stress and to interference from other activities that may be performed concurrently. (Fitts, 1962: 188)

Automatization is usually inferred from the decreasing reliance on exteroceptive sources of feedback. These sources of information become redundant and there is therefore available capacity to 'time-share' and perform a secondary simultaneous task. The extreme case of automatization is Keele's previously mentioned concept of a motor programme which could trigger off responses independent of even proprioceptive feedback. Presumably larger and larger units of behaviour could become programmed as skill progresses.

Hierarchical levels of skill. An examination of many everyday skills demonstrates it is difficult to explain control in terms of one single feedback loop. The operation of a single key on the piano can be characterized by a single feedback system. However this does not help us to understand the richness of the play of the skilled pianist. This activity of pressing a key is only part of the overall system, which may be analysed at either a macro or micro-level. The activity of pressing a single key may itself be viewed as a subordinate element of the activity of, for example, playing a chord which may in turn be part of playing a piece of Chopin. A chord consists of the spatial and temporal organization of a set of notes and itself is part of the organization of the piece of music. Each of these higher level activities may be conceptualised in terms of a single feedback loop. A similar analysis may be extended at the micro-level. Playing a note can be further subdivided into the component operations of moving the hand into position, then moving the relevant finger in the right direction at the right speed etc. Clearly then such skill may be conceptualized as a hierarchical structure of actions organized spatially and temporally on the basis of feedback loops.

Holloway (1974) illustrates how driving a car may be similarly viewed as a series of actions which are controlled by feedback but organized in a hierarchical fashion:

Steering, braking, accelerating, scanning and searching are all activities which can be described in terms of feedback control loops but each activity is meshed into an overall plan which allocates priorities and sequences to these individual behaviours and sets up the rules for overriding one activity with another. A useful integration of the idea of the feedback loop and the hierarchy concept is provided by the nature of a TOTE which is a simplified level of feedback-loop (1974: 34).

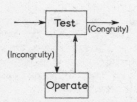

Fig 2.5 *The TOTE unit* (*Miller et al, 1960*)

Miller, Galanter and Pribram (1960) introduced the concept of a TOTE unit which stands for *T*est, *O*perate, *T*est, *E*xit. (Fig. 2.5) The 'Test' phase assesses whether there is any difference between the actual and desired state of the system. If there is a discrepancy then action is performed under the 'operate' phase aimed at resolving this incongruity, and a subsequent 'test' made. This cycle of test, operate, test, continues until any incongruity is eliminated at which time action is terminated via the 'exit' path. Miller, Galanter and Pribram (1960) use the example of hammering a nail to illustrate how TOTEs may be organized hierarchically by a 'plan'. They define a 'plan' as

'any hierarchical process in the organisation that can control the order in which the sequence of operations is to be performed' (p. 16)

A simple TOTE unit will control the process of hammering and is evidence of the existence of a 'plan' for hammering. The 'test' phase determines whether the nail is sufficiently flush with the surface of the material. If it is not, then the action of hammering is performed under the 'operate' phase and again subsequently evaluated in the 'test' phase. This iterative process continues until the nail is flush whence 'exit' indicates that control from the TOTE unit for hammering is relinquished and may pass to a different TOTE. The crucial point is that the operational phase of any TOTE may itself have embedded lower order TOTEs. In the hammering example the operational phase of 'hammer', is itself comprised of two subactivities, that of

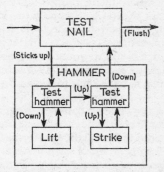

Fig. 2.6 *A TOTE hierarchy (Miller et al, 1960)*

lifting the hammer and that of striking the nail. These two activities will be controlled by two separate TOTE units and organized by the 'plan' for hammering as shown in Fig. 2.6. The overall plan may be 'repair the garden fence'. This could be subdivided into the activities of 'remove the broken wood' and 'replace with new wood'. In turn the latter activity could be further subdivided into the activities of finding, preparing and securing the new wood which must be correctly sequenced by the plan 'replace with new wood'. Eventually the lower level activity of hammering would become evident in such a hierarchical analysis.

The conception of skilled activity as being hierarchically organized and controlled at each level by the feedback loop attached to each TOTE has important implications for training. If task performance is unacceptable, task analysis may

41

proceed most economically from the higher levels until the source of the problem is identified. Poor performance may be a consequence of an inappropriate or ineffective plan, ineffective feedback for the test phase of a TOTE or incorrect sequencing of suboperations in the task. In a number of complex tasks the performer may be guided by an inappropriate plan (at any level of the task). Hence, as Fitts and Adams' theories of skill acquisition imply, there should be an initial intellectualization process in which the performer is given the appropriate verbal plans. In such cases if the trainee is given the most efficient plan, learning and performance will improve considerably. This might be achieved by presenting the trainee with a decision tree or algorithm which details the various courses of action to follow given certain situations. Similarly the 'do-it-yourself' car mechanic could more easily find the fault if given the optimal procedure for eliminating the various alternatives.

In case the reader is still in doubt as to how skilled performance is organized, Fitts and Posner's (1967) computer analogy in which a programme is equivalent to a plan should be helpful:

The opportunity to develop complex programs to govern the operations of large electronic data-processing systems has led to new conceptions of how skilled performance bay be organized in man. The operation of such systems is governed by a program or sequence of instructions. Parts of the program may be repeated over and over again. These short, fixed sequences of operations are written as *subroutines* which may be called into play as units by the overall program. Such subroutines may be repeated over and over again until some predetermined point is reached or until interrupted by the overall program. These fixed sequences are under the control of a higher level or *executive program* which provides the overall logical or decision framework that gives the system its flexible and adaptive characteristic. In much the same way, some sequences of movement become fixed units within complex human activity. These fixed units are quite automatic, and may be incorporated as components in many different activities. The timing and order of these units will vary with different skills and provide the unique character of each activity. Learning skills involves a new integration and ordering of units, many of which may be transferred as a whole from other activities. (1967: 10–11)

Quite simply the acquisition of skill may be viewed as the progressive organization of units of activity into a hierarchical structure. Anecdotal examples can be used to exemplify this view. Consider a person learning to serve in the game of tennis. Initially the task can be divided into the activities of positioning oneself on the baseline, throwing the ball in the air and hitting the ball with the racket. These activities will be adapted initially on the basis of extrinsic feedback from the trainer and the intrinsic feedback from the task. Proprioceptive feedback may be particularly important whilst in the early stages of learning the trainee may also need to watch the ball in order to hit it. The gradual adaption of these activities will occupy considerable processing capacity. The components of serving will become organized both spatially and temporally and be eventually triggered off as a larger unit by the overall plan 'serve' and will be altered only with considerable difficulty. This automatization has been noted by Fitts and will release information processing capacity for other activities. The expert tennis player has more capacity available to consider which type of serve to select and where to place the ball, etc. Furthermore the skilled tennis player will learn to recognize and interpret cues from his opponents and thus to anticipate play. Hence characteristically the skilled performer has so much more time than the unskilled player.

It is worth mentioning an experiment, examining the temporal organization of a skill, by Pew (1966), which provides rare confirmation for these ideas. The task involved maintaining a target at a central position whilst successively pressing two keys which effected acceleration of the target to the left and right. Early in training, control was poor because interresponse times were long. Pew states:

These records are suggestive of a closed loop mode of operation in which S responded, waited for feedback about the results of this response and then initiated a new response intended to compensate for the inadequacies of the last previous one. (1966:769)

In other words the activities involved in the task had not been integrated in time such that they could be triggered automatically. In the later stages of training interresponse time decreased and two distinct strategies emerged. The poorer subjects seemed to pause occasionally in a series of rapid presses to make a correction. Subjects who improved more rapidly gradually corrected any drift of the target by depressing one key slightly longer than the other. Generally then throughout training the task had been organized at progressively higher levels which meant that the lags associated with correction on the basis of feedback for individual movements were gradually eliminated.

3
Analysis for training

In the previous chapter skill acquisition was viewed as a process of *synthesis* of lower level activities into an integrated hierarchy of skilled performance. Training therefore must endeavour to encourage such a synthesis. In order to do this the trainer must gain an understanding of the task to be performed. This understanding must be in terms of what the component activities of the task are, and what demands, psychologically, they will place on the trainee. In other words some *analysis* of the task needs to precede the design of training for it. In Chapter 1, a systems view of training (Fig. 1.1) was outlined. Its initial component is 'define training objectives', i.e. what is the goal of performance of the task? From this first stage criterion measures can be devised to 'test' trained people. The content of the training programme is also derived from this. All of this activity can be subsumed under the general heading of *task analysis*. The aim is to ascertain what the objectives of the task are, how these objectives can be met, and what the nature of the information processing demands will be on the performer in the attainment of these objectives.

An examination of the training literature and discussions with people in the field, reveal that genuine difficulties exist over terminology. This is perhaps most apparent in the case of the processes of analysing activities to derive the training content. The terms Job, Task and Skill Analysis might be used interchangeably or to represent different processes or even to refer to different stages within the same process. Fortunately these different terms typically refer to the same process, that of identifying the training needs and determining the training content. It should be recognized however that the term 'job analysis' does have wider connotations in occupational psychology, for example, for personnel selection and job evaluation. It is, of course, widely accepted that some examination of the tasks should be carried out in órder to determine what should constitute an appropriate training course. It is also accepted that this involves a description and a breakdown of the tasks into elements of some kind. However no such general agreement exists as to how this should be accomplished as there are a number of very different approaches and techniques which may be adopted.

Job analysis is probably the most commonly used term in industry. Under this heading *one* method of analysis is often described. It is, however, also used as a generic term under which various methods are subsumed. The *Glossary of Training Terms* defines it as, 'The process of examining a job in detail in order to identify its component tasks. The detail and approach may vary according to the purpose for which the job is being analysed e.g. training, equipment design, work lay-out.'

It can be seen that wider aspects of activity than that relevant to training are covered by this definition. Thus Singleton (1967) uses the term job to refer to 'the overall unified activities of the operator' indicating that it is 'an operator oriented term'. Similarly Annett *et al* (1971) state that 'Job is thus a person-oriented concept, it usually has a title and contractual implications. These and other personnel considerations, on the basis of which tasks are assigned to jobs, will not be our concern, rather we shall address ourselves to *tasks*, as such, and the problem of determining their training implications.'

For training purposes therefore the more specific term of *task analysis* is preferred. Task analysis in the *Glossary of Training Terms* is 'A systematic analysis of the behaviour required to carry out a task with a view to identifying areas of difficulty and the appropriate training techniques and learning aids necessary for successful instruction'.

Task analysis is seen therefore both as a process of collecting information on task behaviour, and as a method indicating the necessary training. Annett *et al* (1971) emphasise that such an analysis should be an all-embracing activity, the end product of which should not only be a description of behaviour, but also

should form the basis for the design of the training programme.

> The most general way of looking at task analysis is as the
> process of collecting information necessary to reach decisions
> about what to train, how to train, even how well to train, and
> perhaps how much to spend on training. In short task analysis
> should lead *directly* to a training design specifying not only
> what is usually called 'course content' but also the output or
> criterion performance and the method or methods of training
> by which this can be achieved. (1971 : 1)

This approach to task analysis will be adopted and described in
further detail in this chapter.

The term *skills analysis* is used in two ways. Firstly as a
synonym for job or task analysis, and secondly for the specific
technique or analysis which has been described by Seymour
(1966). In the former case emphasis is placed, during analysis,
on the perceptual-motor aspects of the tasks in question, often
leading to recording in great detail. Seymour's technique is a
development of this approach whereby actions are recorded,
together with information on which limb used, etc. Emphasis is
placed, quite rightly, on the perceptual aspects of the task, i.e.
the cues used by the operator, both for input and feedback.
Such an approach is limited mostly to those tasks that may be
called 'skilled' in that they are basically manual tasks. Later in
this chapter a task analysis technique which claims generality of
application is described. This latter technique does not preclude
the use of detailed skills analysis. A compromise therefore would
be to see *jobs* as made up of *tasks*. The tasks may need to be
performed with more or less *skill* depending on their context,
and require analysis in more or less detail.

Taxonomies

The process of analysis can be aided by the use of classification
schemes which enable the analyst to categorize the various
activities that he isolates. The development of such a taxonomy
has often been advocated as the key to understanding skilled
performance. However the usefulness of any taxonomy clearly
depends on its purpose or objectives. Different taxonomies may

be constructed for different purposes, a fact which is not often adequately recognized. A review of taxonomies for training by Annett and Duncan (1967) emphasizes that one criterion is that the categories must be mutually exclusive and exhaustive. The additional major criterion is that the categories should specify different training characteristics. The utility of any taxonomy is therefore totally dependent on the relevance and usefulness of the categories for the purpose of training rather than the elegance of the taxonomic scheme.

The history of such approaches began with work study techniques which classified elements of work such as 'grasp', 'locate', etc. Work study techniques do not analyse skill in a way relevant to training problems. What essentially are recorded are sequences of movements and their nature. These isolated elements can then be assigned predetermined time values. One point that is made with these methods is that if such an analysis is to be useful for training, additional information, such as 'job knowledge', is required. Even with this, work study would seem to have limited applicability to the majority of tasks, as Conrad (1951) has pointed out: 'relatively casual observation and use of instruments which reveal nothing but overt bodily movements are likely to lead to concepts of skill which are extremely vulnerable.' Thus we are in danger of leaving out essential considerations of perception, anticipation, decision making, etc. A system to complement work study is provided by Crossman (1956), which records decisions to be made, senses used, etc. as well as the motions carried out. Unfortunately although the technique is well documented it seems mostly appropriate for repetitive manual tasks, and also little indication is given on how a training programme may be derived from such an analysis.

A taxonomy which does put emphasis on the psychological demands of tasks is that of R. B. Miller (1967). Miller asks, what functions would have to be built into a robot to make him behave like a human being performing a particular task? He lists the following categories:

Concept of purpose
A function which could be programmed so that sooner or later he could discriminate relevant from irrelevant cues, responses and feedback, and to enable him to be turned 'on' by inciting cues and turned 'off' by criterion-matching cues.

Concepts of purpose may be single-values (such as reeling off a programmed procedure to a predictable series of cues) or multiple-valued (such as in inductive decision making). This 'concept of purpose' function, by the way, is the most difficult to design into a box.

Scanning function
Active or passive search for exposing his perceptive apparatus to task-inciting cues in the environment, or to cues generated by himself.

Identification of relevant cues function
A function whereby he identifies or differentiates a pattern of cues as a pattern either from a background or noise or from other patterns of cues. A label or some other discriminatory action would be attached to the identifying operation.

Interpretation of cues
Interpretation according to the 'meaning' or implication apart from the physical nature of the cue itself.

Short-term memory
For holding together, during a task cycle, the fragments of information that will be acted upon later or combined into a clump. This function is much broader than apperception span, by the way. It operates as extensively and as elaborately as the continuation of my concept of purpose and my recall of what I have said during this presentation.

Long-term memory
The case of recallable associations between and among stimuli and responses. The associations may be automatic perceptual-motor, or they may be symbolic in cognitive awareness. In relatively simple form, long-term memory is seen in strict precedural performance. But memory may also consist of trains of symbolic associations, such as images of a map or a terrain.

Decision making and problem solving
Techniques which may be divergent and convergent, computational or strategic, and so on; a trade off against long-term memory (or 'table lookup'): response selection or formulation

in the absence of a sufficiently dominant association between the cue pattern, the response pattern and the concept of purpose. Problem solving requires information provided by the functions already mentioned plus processing by strategy rules or concepts with symbolic response repertoires. Decision making and problem solving can be useful divided into further categories.

Effector response
The outputs that do work on the environment, including symbolic work. (Miller, 1967: 171–172)

This technique puts emphasis on the kinds of activity being performed and their demands on the human operator. Different types of activity will have different implications for training. So as the analysis proceeds, using such an approach, different training requirements will emerge. But Miller does not directly relate different training methods to each category. Rather, he uses them to suggest that training for different functions will proceed separately as training exercises.

A different kind of taxonomy has been developed by Gagné (1970) which distinguishes behaviour in terms of eight different categories of learning. (see A3)

Type 1 Signal Learning. The individual learns to make a general, diffuse response to a signal. This is the classical conditioned response of Pavlov....

Type 2 Stimulus-Response Learning. The learner acquires a precise response to a discriminated stimulus. What is learned is a connection ..... or a discriminated operant ..... sometimes called an instrumental response......

Type 3 Chaining. What is acquired is a chain of two or more stimulus-response connections. The conditions for such learning have been described by Skinner......

Type 4 Verbal Association. Verbal association is the learning of chains that are verbal. Basically, the conditions resemble those for other (motor) chains. However, the presence of language in the human being makes this a special type because internal links may be selected from the individual's previously learned repertoire of language......

Type 5 Discrimination Learning. The individual learns to make *n* different identifying responses to as many different stimuli, which may resemble each other in physical appearance to a greater or lesser degree. Although the learning of each stimulus-response connection is a simple type 2 occurrence, the connections tend to interfere with each other's retention......

Type 6 Concept Learning. The learner acquires a capability of making a common response to a class of stimuli that may differ from each other widely in physical appearance. He is able to make a response that identifies an entire class of objects or events.... Other concepts are acquired *by definition*, and consequently have the formal characteristics of rules.

Type 7 Rule Learning. In simplest terms, a rule is a chain of two or more concepts. It functions to control behaviour in the manner suggested by a verbalized rule of the form, 'if A, then B,' where A and B are previously learned concepts. However, it must be carefully distinguished from the mere verbal sequence, 'If A, then B,' which, of course, may also be learned as type 4.

Type 8 Problem Solving. Problem solving is a kind of learning that requires the internal events usually called thinking. Two or more previously acquired rules are somehow combined to produce a new capability that can be shown to depend on a 'higher-order' rule. (Gagné, 1970: 63–64)

Some of these categories clearly overlap with those in Miller's taxonomy. Gagné's scheme is novel since the categories are arranged hierarchically. For example, concept learning is most efficient if the necessary discrimination learning precedes it. This technique is a more sophisticated attempt to relate categories of behaviour to not only their learning requirements but also a sequence of learning. (See p. 81)

Hierarchical task analysis

An analysis technique, which can be applied to a wide range of tasks, has been developed at the University of Hull. Hierarchical task analysis is probably its best name and the process is outlined by Annett and Duncan (1967). Tasks are broken down into 'operations' which are the units of analysis. These are similar to the TOTE units proposed by G. A. Miller *et al* (1960) discussed in the previous chapter. Operations are defined as: 'any unit of behaviour, no matter how long or short its duration and no matter how simple or complex its structure, which can be defined in terms of its objective.' (Annett *et al.*, 1971) The key to this technique is the operation which is identified with a behavioural unit. This focuses attention on the objectives of the task rather than just the activity being performed. It also should free us from any prejudice about the number of levels of description required in any analysis. Operations can be broken down into suboperations, and these can again be subdivided. With such a general unit as the operation, no assumptions need to be made at the initiation of any analysis of how many levels of breakdown are necessary. Thus inherent flexibility is its main advantage over some techniques which assume a simple level of analysis throughout, i.e. a technique which simply records 'elements', or else others which prescribe a fixed number of levels of analysis, e.g. tasks, activities and elements.

The concept of the operation can be applied to a wide variety of tasks, in order to develop hierarchical descriptions of them which will give more or less detail depending on the context of the analysis. Let us now examine aspects of hierarchical task analysis in more detail. In Fig. 3.1 the three components of an operation and their relationship to the operator or person performing them are presented. During the analysis of each operation it is necessary to isolate:—

Input: signals or cues in the environment which tell the person to perform the operation

Action: the appropriate behaviour which needs to be performed during the operation

Feedback: signals or cues which tell the operator how adequate his actions are, and if he has completed the operation.

52

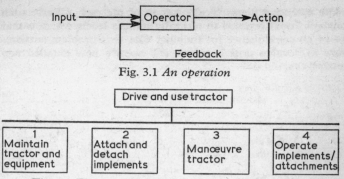

Fig. 3.1 *An operation*

Fig. 3.2 *First stage of a task analysis of tractor driving*

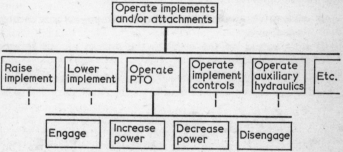

Fig. 3.3 *Partial further breakdown of operation 4 of tractor driving*

This entails a closer examination of tasks and their psychological demands. Whilst the description of the operation is simply a statement of its objectives, the analysis in terms of input, action and feedback begins to specify these demands. It also should record what is necessary in training for successful performance of the operation i.e. preparing people to meet those demands.

Analysis of a task in terms of operations should proceed hierarchically. The overall objectives of the task from the first operation. Let us use an example of the tractor driver. In Fig. 3.2 the operation 'drive and use tractor' represents the overall objectives of a tractor driver. This operation can be broken down into four subordinate operations, which give more detail. Each of these can be analysed further, as in Fig. 3.3, to give a more extensive hierarchical diagram of the task. Clearly such analysis could proceed to absurdly minute levels which would be of no consequence for training. The next problem is therefore to develop criteria which will specify how detailed any analysis should be.

Criteria for analysis

Previously it was mentioned that the degree of detail would depend very much on the context. Many techniques assume that analysts will use rules of thumb like, 'give more detail with critical tasks', or 'give attention to areas of special difficulty'. Whilst such rules may be useful, they are apt to be too vague and lacking in general applicability. In hierarchical analysis, Annett and Duncan (1967) suggest that as each operation is isolated two questions should be asked of it:

(i) what is the probability *without* training of inadequate performance?
(ii) what would be the costs to the system of inadequate performance?

If the best available estimates of these values, or rather their *product*, is unacceptable, then the performance in question is redescribed in more detail, i.e. broken down into subordinate operations and each of these is then submitted in turn to the same decision rule. In some cases it will be necessary to redescribe several times in increasing detail, in others not. The analysis ceases, either when the values specified in the rule are acceptable to the system, or when training requirements for adequate performance are clear. (Annett and Duncan, 1967: 212)

The first question is directed at determining how likely, with a given trainee population, performance will be acceptable without training. In other words will a simple instruction suffice, or is more detail, i.e. further analysis, necessary? Using our tractor example, a specific piece of equipment is the power take-off (PTO), which is a means of powering equipment attached behind a tractor. From Fig. 3.3 the statement 'operate PTO' is not sufficient detail for adequate performance, but subordinate to this, the statement 'increase power' will give sufficient information to the majority of trainees. This is a first step towards putting analysis and training into its context. The aspects considered here are the previous levels of training and the abilities and aptitudes of the trainees. If people are being recruited for a job which involves a new machine performing an old process, then the analyst will probably need to provide more detail for training school leavers for the tasks than for the operators of the old process. This estimate of the *probability* of failure for each operation is represented by P.

The second question places the operation into its costs context. Some operations need little or no training and some can be learned quickly in the job situation. Designing a training programme for some operations may cost more than it saves in lost production and inefficiency. On the other hand there may be very critical operations, which although simple may carry high financial penalties if performed inadequately. The *cost* value is represented by C.

The decision rule on redescription is then to combine P and C in a multiplicative fashion ($P \times C$), and if the value is unacceptable to the system, then the operation can be further analysed. In this context the system refers to the environment in which the training specialist is working, the objectives he has been set, and the resources available to him. The multiplicative rule is used because if either the value of P or C is at or near zero, then their product also will be at or near zero. This therefore gives a quick indication of operations which are not critical or which present little learning difficulty. The $P \times C$ rule is applied to each operation in turn. Again if the value obtained is unacceptable, then that operation is further broken down, and the rule applied to each subordinate operation. This will most likely yield a large, irregular block diagram, but one in which only the essential operations will be represented.

Rules for sequencing operations
When an operation is broken down into subordinate operations the analyst must state how the subordinates are ordered. In other words he must state the rule governing the sequencing or selection of subordinates. Some operations are performed serially and follow very simple rules, such as, 'do A, then B, then C, etc.' Others involve performing two or more operations concurrently or in close temporal proximity. For example the tractor driver often has both to 'manoeuvre tractor' and 'operate implements' at the same time. With other operations, on the other hand, no particular order may exist. For example, a traffic warden must be able to 'give parking tickets', 'direct

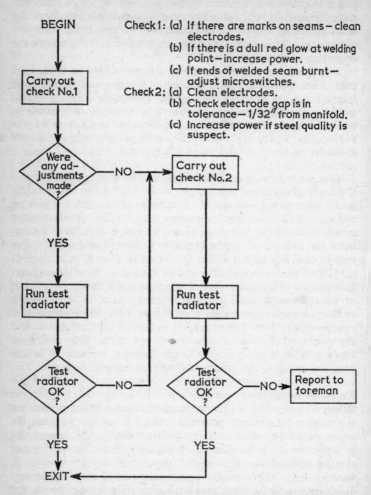

Fig. 3.4 *Decision tree for selecting suboperations when leaking radiators are reported* (From Annett *et al.*, 1971)

traffic' and 'give directions to pedestrians', etc. There will be an order of priorities for these operations, but no actual predetermined sequence of them which is intrinsic to the job. In many tasks the sequence of operations is a branching one, one operation may lead to two or more alternatives. Fig. 3.4 presents the sequence for locating faults in the particular industrial process of radiator welding. A number of decisions have to be made, and particular sequences are dependent upon the outcome of each question. A decision tree or algorithm is a particularly useful way of recording this type of rule structure. The rule must be recorded when the operation is broken down. If any of the subordinate operations are further analysed then again *rules* of *sequence* or *selection* should be stated.

Recording the analysis
We have progressed this far without discussing how exactly information can be recorded. This is because whilst recording techniques are important, the general approach of the analyst is more important than the format of recording. Nevertheless some guidelines on recording can be given, although fuller expositions can be found in Annett *et al.* (1971) and Duncan (1972). The hierarchical diagram is useful for showing the structure of the task, but limited in its capacity for recording detailed information. It should be used in conjunction with a table, recording the name of the operation, or perhaps just assigning a reference number. The table consists of a number of columns, as shown in Fig. 3.5, where the first stages of an analysis of fencing by J. P. Davies (1972) is presented. In the first column are the reference numbers to the diagram. The second, and most important column, contains a statement of the operation which is always in terms of an instruction to perform the operation. Also included in this column are the training comments, with suitable prefixes, which describe the rules for sequencing suboperations (R), together with input (I), action (A) or feedback (F) difficulties. Any further training comment can also be made here, as well as possible training solutions (see next section). The final columns serve to indicate whether any difficulties exist in the operation, and if it is broken down, the numbers of suboperations. At the conclusion of the analysis, the table will contain:

(*a*) a list of all operations, as instructions

57

No.	Description of Operation and Training Notes	I/F	A	Redescribed
1	Fence with the sabre. $\boxed{R.}$ Convention means an invariant order. 1,1 to 1,3. Score a hit on the target of the opponent without getting hit oneself within the rules. Must learn the convention—possibly fencing films.	–	x	1,1 – 1,3
1,1	Attack the opponent. $\boxed{R.}$ Invariant order 1,1,1 to 1,1,3 although 1,1,1 (the grip) is maintained throughout the fight. The target is anywhere above the waist of the opponent including the arms. Once indicated this should be clear; may be helped by colouring the target area.	–	x	1,1,1 – 1,1,3
1,2	Defend an opponent's attack. $\boxed{R.}$ Always 1,2,1 but defence may be by either evasion (1,2,2) or by parrying (1,2,3) $\boxed{I.}$ The choice of alternative depends on the amount of pressure in the fight and upon the strengths and weaknesses of the opponent and is thus specific to each fight. Evasion should not be encouraged because it does not earn the right to attack.	x	x	1,2,1 – 1,2,3
1,3	Reply to opponent's attack. $\boxed{R.}$ Operation 1,3,1 and 1,3,2 are wholly time shared but the type of hit (1,3,2) will vary from one riposte to another. All ripostes follow a parry by the rules of fencing.	–	x	1,3,1 – 1,3,2

Fig. 3.5 *Extract from a task analysis table of fencing*

(b) the rules for sequencing suboperations (an additional decision tree may be useful here)
(c) notes on difficulties
(d) training comment.

This will provide all the inputs for the next components in the training system, 'designing methods and media' and 'developing criterion measures' (see Fig. 1.1).

Training alternatives
The transition from task analysis to training design is not, however, a simple translation process. There will often be alternative methods of training (which are discussed in later chapters), and one training method may not be readily apparent at the time of analysis. All these alternatives, and ideas, no matter how vague, can be noted in the table at the time of analysis. They will have to be considered in the training design stage. The number and feasibility of these alternatives depends both on the level of development of the pertinent training research and the degree of familiarity of the task analyst with it. Nevertheless, such comments should be attempted, particularly when the real task situation is being viewed.

Another alternative which should be considered is whether to train or not to train. If lists of instructions or decision trees have been considered then they could be used not only for training, but also to supplant training, by supporting performance with what are called 'job aids' (Wulff & Berry, 1962). This is an important decision because very different kinds of performance may result. Even with the best designed training scheme occasional human errors may still occur. Job aids may be helpful in overcoming this problem. However their disadvantages need to be appreciated. They may function primarily as temporary crutches to performance and their removal or the transfer to a related task may reveal no underlying learning gains by the trainee. Such a decision, whether to train or use job aids, must depend on context and sometimes will depend on non-training considerations such as management preferences (see Duncan, 1972: 69–71 for further discussion of this area).

Sources of information
There are many methods of collecting task information and an analysis in any particular situation can utilize one or more of them.

Existing documentation. This can cover previous analyses, e.g. for work study. Operating manuals, maintenance guides, rules and previous training manuals can be useful. Accident reports may also point to critical operations.

Observation. Simple observations with note taking can cover a multitude of situations. Photographic records, with the potential for fast or slow motion recording, extend observational power. Closed-circuit television is a very convenient form of visual recording, with a sound channel usually being available as well. The analyst can resort to practice of the task himself for further insight into the task demands. For some tasks continual observation may be necessary whilst for others, activity sampling can be sufficient. Task performance can be accompanied by a verbal description of the process.

Interviews. Questions can be informally asked of the task performer during observation. Information may be spontaneously given, or it can be collected in a structured or unstructured interview situation. The *Critical Incident Technique*, outlined by Flanagan (1954), collects information on near accidents and critical or particularly difficult operations, which may be, or at least should be, very rare.

Simulation. In this context the word simulation represents any model of the real life situation used for analysis purposes rather than training. Various kinds of simulation can be practised in order to both generate and validate information. These can range from full scale simulations of systems to paper and pencil exercises. Simulations are necessary for a variety of reasons: (a) In the development of new systems where the tasks do not exist; (b) For the validation of information collected from operators. For example Duncan (1972) reports that even the most experienced operators did not use optimal strategies for fault detection in a chemical process. The optimal strategy was derived from a logical decision tree analysis of the task. (c) Examination of some task situations may be dangerous. In a study of air traffic controllers Laplat and Bisseret (1966) presented simulated situations to them and studied the strategies adopted.

This brief overview of sources of information is not exhaustive. Our aim is to show that a range of approaches exists where the chief criterion must be utility, validity and reliability in collecting information about the task. Further details can be found in basic texts (e.g. Chapanis, 1959; Blum & Naylor, 1968).

Conclusions

The method of hierarchical task analysis has been advocated in this chapter, since it is general in its approach, and has been applied to a range of tasks. However there are a number of alternative methods (see Annett and Duncan, 1967). The chief criterion for any analysis method must be that it leads to positive training recommendations. In addition it should be economic in its approach to data collection and in harmony with current thinking in psychology on how human performance is represented. In order to gain a more detailed understanding of task analysis the reader may now find it helpful to attempt to analyse a simple everyday task.

4
Feedback and guidance

Chapter 2 discussed the theoretical background of skill acquisition. These ideas suggest particular techniques for increasing the efficiency of learning skills. The level of skilled performance is generally measured by the attributes of *speed* and
accuracy. Research on techniques for training skill emphasizes
the efficiency of different ways of presenting information to the
trainee about these two attributes. The model of skilled performance described in Chapter 2 emphasizes the important role
of feedback during the learning process. Such feedback can be
either *intrinsic* or *extrinsic* to the task. Part of this chapter
investigates feedback that is extrinsic i.e. supplementary to the
information inherent in the normal task situation and which will
eventually be removed. This is the most common method of
presenting information concerning the attributes of speed and
accuracy which the trainee must obtain to become skilled. The
remainder of this chapter examines alternative techniques for
presenting such information, namely *guidance*, *prompting* and
cuing. More detailed reviews are available of extrinsic feedback
(Adams, 1971), whilst a more theoretical discussion is presented
by Annett (1969). Extrinsic feedback provides the learner with
information on his performance. Such feedback may be *concurrent* with performance or occur at its *termination*. Guidance
and cuing give the learner *advance* or *concurrent* information
as to what performance is required. For example, the trainee
for an industrial inspection task may be told in advance that a
flaw will be present in the next item he sees, or a gymnast may

be manually guided through a movement. We shall firstly consider varieties of extrinsic feedback, secondly the effects of their manipulation on learning and finally guidance and related techniques will be examined.

Varieties of extrinsic feedback

The range of techniques is organized into the following pairs of alternatives by Holding (1965).

Concurrent or terminal. As mentioned above, extrinsic feedback occurs either during or after the execution of a response. For example, in training a missile operator an auditory and/or visual signal may be given to indicate when he is on target. This would constitute concurrent feedback. On the other hand, a summary score, indicating accuracy, may be delivered after an attempt at guiding the missile. This would be terminal feedback. This dichotomy is however misleading because for such continuously adjustive responses as above, the concurrent feedback in fact refers to part of the response sequence which has been *previously* executed. In this sense it may be pedantically described as *terminal* to parts of the total response sequence. Therefore when feedback is termed concurrent the use only refers to the occurrence of feedback during performance of the task and does not imply that feedback occurs simultaneously with the part of the sequence to which it refers.

Immediate or delayed. Extrinsic feedback necessarily occurs after a response, as mentioned above. The dichotomy between immediate and delayed is convenient to distinguish feedback given directly when a response is completed, from feedback occurring after some noticeable interval. Such a delay may be a consequence either of an inherent equipment lag and/or an intentional delay.

Verbal or non-verbal. Any form of extrinsic feedback can be given in some verbal form, e.g. a statement of an error score in millimetres. Alternatively the information can be displayed in some non-verbal form, e.g. the visual or auditory signals in the above missile example.

Separate or accumulated. Scores can be given separately following each attempt at a task, or given at the end of a series of attempts, as a *summary* or *average* score.

Extrinsic feedback in any situation can be classified on the basis of each dichotomy. Thus immediate, verbal, separate, terminal feedback or non-verbal concurrent feedback are possible varieties. Different combinations have yielded differences in efficiency, although it is difficult to generalize because of the limited range of tasks studied under various conditions of feedback. Any particular task will have an optimal method, although in practice it may be difficult to determine. Nevertheless the next section will attempt to formulate some general guidelines.

Studies of manipulations of extrinsic feedback

This section gives a brief coverage of some of the most important findings associated with extrinsic feedback and the reader should consult the references given at the beginning of this chapter for greater detail. The effect of presence or absence, specificity, delay, timing of withdrawal and different types of extrinsic feedback will be examined.

Presence or absence of extrinsic feedback

The question whether extrinsic feedback is necessary for learning initiated the study of this area. Thorndike (1927) compared rates of learning to draw lines of specified lengths, whilst blindfold. Hardly surprising, subjects given no feedback failed to improve with respect to the criterion distance, despite many attempts. Other subjects did learn when given feedback in terms of 'right' or 'wrong' which indicated whether an attempt was within plus or minus one quarter inch of the target. This study demonstrated that no learning occurs in relation to the criterion, but a re-examination of Thorndike's original data found an improvement in the consistency of subjects' attempts. 'Learning' in a sense occurred, presumably as a consequence of the more efficient utilization of the *intrinsic* proprioceptive feedback, although the development of a motor programme remains a possibility.

Specificity of extrinsic feedback

The study of Trowbridge and Cason (1932), besides supporting

Thorndike's results, also demonstrated an advantage of quantitative feedback. Subjects given quantitative feedback, in units of one-eighth of an inch, reached higher levels of accuracy than those only told 'right' or 'wrong' depending on whether an attempt was within one eighth of an inch of the target. This result led to further research on the relationship between specificity of feedback and the rate of learning. For example, McGuigan (1959) used three levels of specificity, telling subjects 'correct' if any attempt was within one, five or ten eighths of an inch of the target in a hand positioning task. Amount of learning was greater with more specific feedback. However, Annett (1969) reports an unpublished experiment in which subjects. engaged in a lever pulling task, were given feedback on a three, seven or sixty point scale. There was no difference in rate of learning, and Annett suggests that there is a limit to the amount of feedback information which can be utilized in learning. This proposition has been substantiated by a number of studies showing no improvement in rate of learning with more precise feedback (e.g. Smoll, 1971). A study by Rogers (1974), whilst finding an improvement in learning over three increasingly precise feedback conditions, found that learning was considerably inhibited when a fourth, more detailed, condition was used. If, however, the time interval between feedback and execution of the next response was increased, then the inhibition disappeared. This is consistent with the concept of a limited information handling capacity, and suggests that, given more time, the learner can utilize more information. The advice for the trainer would be to attempt to ascertain the optimum level of specificity of feedback useful for a particular task.

Delay in extrinsic feedback
The results of an experiment by Greenspoon and Foreman (1956) showed that delay of extrinsic feedback retarded the rate of learning although subsequent experiments have failed to find such an effect (McGuigan, 1959). Bilodeau (1966) suggests that the interresponse interval determines learning rather than the delay itself. In experiments such as these, there are three temporal intervals that can be varied, as shown in Fig. 4.1. Studies where interresponse interval is held constant and delay of extrinsic feedback varied also necessarily vary the post-feedback interval.

There is some evidence (e.g. Dyal, 1966) that the effect of

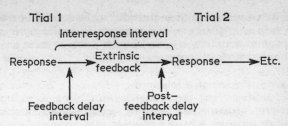

Fig. 4.1 *Temporal sequence in learning*
(After Adams, 1971)

delay is to change the directional bias of the subject when attempting to recall a movement extent. However the evidence is more certain on the effect of delaying feedback by trials. Welford (1968) states that considerable disruption of learning can occur if feedback on a response is only given after subsequent responses.

Withdrawal of extrinsic feedback
A defining feature of extrinsic feedback is that at some stage during or at the end of training it is removed. The effects of withdrawal of extrinsic feedback will depend upon the level of learning of the task. Both Adams' and Fitts' theories of skill acquisition suggest that at some stage extrinsic feedback is no longer relevant to learning. Not surprisingly the evidence is that removal of feedback early in learning has a more disruptive effect than if it is withdrawn later (see Adams, 1971). One example of this is a study by Bilodeau and Bilodeau (1958) in which under one condition feedback was given after every tenth response. Early in practice performance deteriorated after the trial on which feedback was eliminated, but after about sixty trials performance was maintained after the feedback trial. Withdrawal of extrinsic feedback may even be desirable at some stages of practice in order to force the learner to utilize the intrinsic feedback of the task, which is necessary after training. The Bilodeau study demonstrated that learning was proportional to the total number of extrinsic feedback trials, irrespective of their distribution over trials. Thus one hundred trials with feedback on every tenth trial were equivalent to ten trials with feedback on every trial.

The implications for training of this work on feedback withdrawal would appear to be to provide feedback early in training but to fade it gradually as the response becomes more established, and to withdraw it completely at a stage where learning is maintained without feedback.

Concurrent and terminal feedback

This topic has already been discussed in Chapter 2, p. 3 under the heading 'action versus learning' feedback. To summarize, concurrent extrinsic feedback training may produce unwanted effects when withdrawn. To provide an example, if the extrinsic feedback magnifies the extent of the movement, then subjects may overshoot the movement on transfer to the non-feedback condition. This does not mean that *visual* concurrent extrinsic feedback will always lead to poor learning. Both Fox and Levy (1969) and Robb (1972) produce evidence to show that learning can occur under such conditions. The important determining factor is that the visual feedback given to 'guide' movements during training should bear a one-to-one relationship with the movement.

Conclusions on feedback

The studies reviewed here suggest some training guidelines governing the use of feedback. It is necessary for efficient learning but should not be too detailed. Delay of feedback is of little consequence as long as it occurs before the next response and can be withdrawn later in learning. Concurrent extrinsic feedback must be used with care. In order for the learner to develop an efficient 'plan' information about his performance *must* be supplied. The information that is *extrinsic* in training must direct the learner to the information that is *intrinsic* to the task, and which must eventually be used for improving or maintaining performance. The traditional role of extrinsic feedback or 'knowledge of results' has been to provide this information contingent on the learner's performance. There are other techniques which provide task-relevant information and effect learning and are described in the next section.

Guidance

The classic learning paradigm of stimulus – response – reinforcement, focuses attention upon the consequences of responses, i.e. reinforcement, or what is preferably termed extrinsic feedback. Previously the role of feedback in learning has been emphasized. However, it is possible to train skills using techniques which *guide* the learner rather than providing him with information after an attempt at the task. The earliest studies in this area concerned the effects of guiding animals through mazes. This was achieved by blocking blind alleys and more recently by passively transporting the animals through the maze. Generally guidance produced a saving in learning time compared with 'trial and error' techniques. The use of guidance has not received much attention in human learning until recently, probably because it is difficult to explain learning by guidance in the framework of classical learning theory.

Guidance has been termed 'error-free' training, because errors are prevented from occurring during learning by various means. This is important in the light of evidence that errors early in learning tend to be repeated and therefore some of the learning of a task is concerned with 'unlearning' these errors (Holding, 1970). The general term guidance describes a range of 'error-free' techniques. Sometimes its usage is confined to motor tasks, with prompting and cuing describing techniques used in verbal and perceptual tasks.

Types of guidance
Physical restriction. Some device allows active movement but restricts it to the correct path, e.g. blind alleys blocked in mazes or extent of movement delimited by a stop.

Forced response. The required movement is passively executed. The appropriate limbs are moved by some external force, e.g. the subject may hold a stylus which is pulled through the maze.

Visual guidance. The learner can be shown the nature of the movements required and/or the path which they follow.

Verbal guidance. The learner can be instructed about the general nature of the task, appropriate actions, or can be cautioned when error seems imminent.

Evaluation of guidance

Work on the effects of guidance was initiated by Carr and associates in the nineteen twenties. Typically subjects learning a maze were given different numbers of guidance trials and then transferred to an error feedback condition, with practice continuing until some criterion was attained. The general conclusion of Carr (1930) was that small amounts of guidance early in training were particularly effective. However the conclusion that increasing amounts of guidance lead to a decrease in efficiency has been questioned by Holding (1965) on the grounds that the index of efficiency used by Carr will necessarily be biased in this direction. The usual measure of efficiency is to compare control and guided subjects, on transfer to the normal performance condition, following an equal number of trials under each condition.

It is pointed out by von Wright (1957) that the apparent limited effectiveness of large amounts of guidance might be due to the nature of the task to be learned. During restrictive guidance for maze learning, the learner receives information about the correct path and no information about where the choice points are. This limits what can be learned about the maze. It may be that mazes are learned as verbal rather than motor sequences. If the learner has information about the choice points and the alternative wrong responses in advance, the task can be simplified, since movement between choices is unimportant. Its relevant features can be learned and the irrelevant ones ignored. This idea was tested in an experiment by von Wright, (1957) where subjects were required to learn a series of possible left or right responses on a moving display (a type of linear maze). Learning was superior when visual guidance, which showed the subjects the correct path before making a choice, was compared with extrinsic feedback given after the choice. In essence, guidance should be concerned with presenting task-relevant information in the most efficient way. Later work in guidance has concentrated on hand positioning and tracking tasks from which general principles of the efficiency of guidance have emerged.

Tasks which involve learning to move a slider or lever to some criterion have been used to compare guidance with feedback training techniques. Restrictive and mechanical, sometimes termed forced response, guidance were compared with extrinsic feedback by Holding and Macrae (1964). Restrictive guidance, in which the extent of the criterion movement was delimited by a 'stop', was equivalent to feedback training. On the other hand mechanical guidance, in which the subject's hand was pulled to the criterion position, was not as effective as either of the other conditions. The inferiority of forced response training may have been due to the change in conditions from the training to the test situation. This effect may be attributed to a mismatch due to differing proprioceptive feedback from the 'pull' in the guidance training and the 'push' in the test condition or an ineffective execution of a motor programme under changed conditions. Both explanations predict that any difference between the training and test situation will produce poor performance. Conversely training may be more effective when the test conditions are more exactly mimicked. This idea received support from a study by Macrae and Holding (1965a). Mechanical guidance was effective when the movement was executed in a similar fashion under both training and test conditions. Therefore the training recommendation is to use a guidance technique which involves movements most resembling those of the real task.

Guidance has been found superior to feedback with small amounts of training using a lever positioning task (Sulzer and Levy, 1966). This result is hardly surprising since accuracy is particularly poor during the first few attempts with feedback when the subject has little idea of the criterion position. After these initial attempts, there is usually little room for subsequent improvement in performance of the task.

Studies using different tracking tasks found various types of guidance as effective as feedback training. An experiment by Macrae and Holding (1965b) varied amount of mechanical guidance training in a tracking task with two levels of complexity. The results suggested guidance as being more appropriate for more complex tasks, and demonstrated that small amounts of guidance were more effective than larger amounts. A further investigation (Holding and Macrae, 1966) compared the effects of two types of guidance, complete or partial response forcing, given at a fast or slow rate. In complete response forcing, the hand was moved to the target by the equipment, whilst in partial forcing the execution of the incorrect movement was made less probable by the control dynamics. As with positioning tasks, any alteration between the training and test conditions produced poor performance. Thus fast guidance and complete response forcing were less effective training techniques. A final experiment in this series (Macrae and Holding, 1966) found mechanical guidance increasingly advantageous as the complexity of the task increased.

Generally guidance may be a useful training method if it provides relevant response information. Its increased effectiveness in more complex tasks may be that with reduced response uncertainty, available capacity can be used to decipher the difficult perceptual characteristics of the signal.

Prompting

In the area of verbal learning, prompting training techniques have been compared with feedback (confirmation) techniques for paired associate tasks (see A7). In this task, the learner is required to produce a response to a particular stimulus item. For example, post-office letter sorters have to learn to associate a place name with the correct postal district code. Prompting procedures typically involve presenting the trainee with the stimulus and response terms simultaneously, or the response after the stimulus. The trainee may be asked to state the response. The effect of prompting is usually contrasted with extrinsic feedback in which the stimulus is presented, the trainee attempts to respond and is then given the answer. In a review, Aiken and Lau (1967) conclude:

> ... the data indicate that a variety of prompting procedures are equal or superior to a variety of confirmation [feedback] procedures in the learning of verbal paired-associates. The data are contradictory with regard to whether a combined prompting-confirmation procedure yields performance superior to either in pure form, though several researches indicated that prompting is superior to confirmation only early in learning. (1967: 333)

Prompting is most efficient in the initial stages of learning which is comparable to the effect of guidance training.

A perceptual identification task is similar to a verbal paired associate one, in the sense that a name has to be associated with a non-verbal stimulus which might be presented in any modality. Prompting training procedures for perceptual identification differ from their verbal learning counterparts since typically the prompted response name precedes presentation of the stimulus

70

to which it refers. In contrast, under feedback training the subject is presented with the stimulus, attempts to respond and is then given the correct response. Prompting as a training method for identification of complex sounds has a clear advantage. The degree of effectiveness is determined by the amount of overlap between the stimulus and response terms. The effect of prompting in visual identification tasks has been equivocal.

Finally Annett (1966) assessed the effect of prompting for a task requiring the estimation of a number of dots presented tachistoscopically. Prompting was equivalent to feedback training, both of these being superior after training to a control condition in which no information was presented.

Prompting techniques therefore have been found to have general usefulness in verbal and perceptual tasks, although their efficiency in some situations remains unclear. The range of training techniques described for perceptual identification is not exhaustive. For example, studies have shown that the magnification of textile weaves can be a useful training method (Belbin *et al.*, 1957) and that drawing attention to key features assisted the learning of tank identification (Bramley, 1973).

Cuing

This term tends to be restricted to perceptual detection tasks, in which a subject monitors for the occurrence of a signal against a 'noisy' background. Cuing, as a training method, would inform the trainee when a signal is about to occur. Consideration has been given to perceptual tasks in which the stimuli are clearly discriminable, but must be labelled. However, other tasks exist in which, '. . . the subject must learn to respond to low intensity signals occurring at random over the observation interval. Frequently the signals are presented in a noise background' (Aiken and Lau, 1967).

This is commonly termed a signal detection or monitoring task. A typical example would be a radar or sonar detection situation in which the signals may not only be infrequent, but also difficult to detect. Performance of such tasks is indicated by both correct and false detection measures. Aiken and Lau (1967) conclude that training by cuing for auditory detection tasks produces performance that is sometimes superior to feedback. However any superiority is less marked if feedback includes information concerning missed signals. In a review of five auditory detection experiments, Annett and Paterson (1967) conclude,

> Cuing seems to be an effective technique for providing the trainee with instances of the signal about which he can have very little doubt, thus enabling him to build up an image or template against which further instances can be assessed. It enables him, if you like, to build a 'concept' of the signal. This could be achieved, although less efficiently, by knowledge of results. Auditory stimuli of the kind we have been using are ephemeral. By the time the subject learns that that was or was not a signal he has already partly forgotten what he heard. (1967: 426)

They also emphasize that feedback techniques tend to not only increase correct detections but also incorrect responses (i.e. false alarms) whilst cuing heightens sensitivity without undesirable side-effects.

Cuing in *visual* detection tasks appears to have less advantages. Colquhoun (1966) found no differences between cuing and feedback training, and Wiener and Attwood (1968) found the latter method superior. Whilst it is not easy to directly compare studies of visual and auditory detection, a possible explanation of the discrepancy of cuing in visual and auditory detection tasks is that typically the auditory stimuli have been more difficult to discriminate.

Finally cuing has been evaluated as a training method for a task, in which a simple response has to be initiated with respect to a changing visual display, similar to that required of a combat pilot in high speed flight. Prather and Berry (1970) found cuing and feedback equivalent during training, but feedback superior on transfer to performance of a similar task.

Conclusions on guidance, prompting and cuing

The outcome of the research on general 'guidance' techniques is that they are more effective than extrinsic feedback for a range of tasks. The advantages of guidance appear to be, the prevention of error early in learning, the establishment of correct responses, and the presentation of stimulus information in an unambiguous manner. A finding which emerges in a number of cases is their higher rate of efficiency earlier on in practice. Therefore they may be particularly useful in situations where errors made early on in learning could have serious consequences in terms of safety or damage to equipment.

The main disadvantage is that a person may use guidance to support performance and not effect an improvement in learning. Furthermore guidance techniques may become boring to the learner, for example in heavily prompted programmed learning. A practical solution to this dilemma may be to provide an alternation between guidance and extrinsic feedback during training, which would enable guidance to show its effects on the feedback trials and the trainer will therefore know when the trainee has reached the desired level of performance and guidance can be removed. It is surprising that such a 'mixed-mode' of training has received little attention, although Weisz and McElroy (1964) found a combination of prompting and feedback training techniques an advantage in a visual identification task.

The results of research reviewed in this section are encouragingly consistent, although the range of tasks covered is limited. An important point to emerge is that any guidance technique employed should not change the nature of the response demands of the task. Simply supporting error-free performance in training is not sufficient. There is thus a close relationship between task analysis and the selection of an appropriate training method to prepare a trainee for the task's demands.

5
Sequencing of information

Task breakdown or analysis was considered in Chapter 3 whilst in this chapter, various approaches to structuring information for learning will be presented. In common with other areas of training no definitive guidelines exist, and there is a range of possible alternative schemes. The basic problem is one of organizing training so that the optimal sequence of information is presented to the trainee. Some tasks will be so simple that a verbal description and demonstration will suffice. Others will present such a degree of complexity that material has to be presented in a series of discrete chunks. The trainer must then consider what the content of these discrete chunks should be, and their best serial arrangement.

Here we shall consider four areas. Firstly, programmed instruction which is more of a general philosophy for training than a specific approach. The second is Gagné's scheme which uses a particular taxonomy. Finally consideration is given to two enduring debates in the psychology of learning, the part versus whole learning issue and massed versus distributed training.

Programmed instruction

The programmed instruction movement began in the late fifties and early sixties, and has had a large impact on training. Space does not permit a detailed exposition of the background or wider implications of the area (see Kay *et al.*, 1968; Hartley,

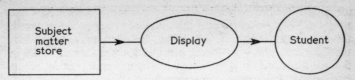

Fig. 5.1 *An open-loop training system (Kay et al, 1963)*

1972b). Its primary importance stemmed from distinguishing the traditional teaching process as an open-loop situation although the ideal learning context is a closed-loop one. These differences are illustrated in Figs. 5.1 and 5.2 by Kay *et al* (1963). In the open-loop situation information is taken from the 'subject matter store', which may be a film, notes or even the instructor's memory and then displayed, visually or aurally, to the student. Such an information processing system is potentially inefficient for a number of reasons. Information may be incorrectly stored, or incorrectly retrieved from the store. The display may be less than adequate and the student or trainee may not be able to absorb the information. With the traditional lecture or talk-with-demonstration any of these faults may be present, but a failure in communication will only be detected if there is a feedback loop which tests whether or not the in-

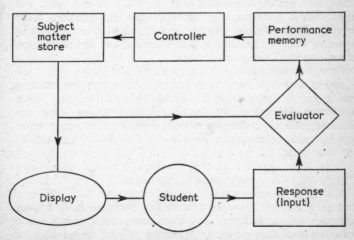

Fig. 5.2 *A closed-loop training system (Kay et al, 1963)*

formation has been absorbed by the learner. Examinations and tests can only partially fulfil this role and anyway are generally too late to remedy any deficiency. In contrast a closed-loop teaching situation puts learning under greater control and Fig. 5.2 demonstrates that several extra components must be incorporated. The extra components are:

Response (input): the learner is asked to make some active response in relation to material which has been presented, e.g. generate an answer to a question, or select from a range of alternative answers.

Evaluator: the response is evaluated in the context of the information presented and the ideal answer.

Performance memory: a store of current and previous responses which is needed for the next component.

Controller: subsequent items of information are selected from the subject matter store on the basis of responses stored in the above component.

The function of selection of information by the 'controller' is a very important one. If the responses have been judged to be acceptable then succeeding information can be presented. On the other hand if errors have been made, or responses are less than adequate then remedial instruction can be provided. This may involve presenting the information in the same or a different form. Instruction can thus be tailored to each individual's learning needs. This is one of the key features of programmed instruction, whereby information is presented on the basis of feedback concerning the learner's progress.

All of these components can be present in a human teaching situation, e.g. the one-to-one tutorial. This can meet the closed-loop requirement but can also be an expensive way of training. Programmed instruction is usually embodied in programmed books, teaching machines, or other devices which present discrete chunks of information and enable responses to be made and recorded. However the hardware is relatively unimportant compared with the structure of the training 'loop' (Fig. 5.2). As long as these important elements are present, the most appropriate methods and devices for the particular training situation can be selected. There are many alternative forms of programmed instruction. Information can be stored and displayed on film, slides or in printed form, or displayed in an auditory form. A response can be written down, selected by a tick or a button push, or may involve perceptual-motor activity. Evaluation may be by the learner, the instructor, or by the programme of a teaching machine. Similarly performance memory and controller functions can be performed by devices or human beings. The reader should appreciate by now that it is difficult to isolate the activity of 'programmed instruction' from other instructional procedures. However programmed instruction does have a consistent functional pattern:

Instruction, or training, is 'programmed' when the subject-matter or content of the course displays the following defining characteristics:
(a) There is a clear-cut statement of objectives, i.e. of 'terminal performance'.
(b) The material to be learned has been itemised and is presented serially in identifiable steps, i.e. frames.
(c) The actual sequence of frames which any student encounters is controlled according to rules derived from the particular programming technique employed.
(d) Frequent and unambiguous responses from every student are required throughout the whole sequence.
(e) Feedback of information about the correctness or otherwise of responses is given to the student before the next frame is presented.
(f) A 'response comparator' is implicit in (e) above to judge between actual and desired (i.e. 'correct') responses. This function can be performed by the student or by a device. (Wallis *et al*, 1966:2)

In the above (a) reemphasises that the objectives of training should be clearly stated which was stressed in Chapter 3. The construction of 'frames' (b) is a difficult aspect of programme writing. Various schemes exist for itemising information, and the reader is referred to I. K. Davies (1972a) for a fuller account. The sequence of frames (c) is intrinsically related to (b). Some programmes have *linear* sequences in which the same order of frames is followed by all learners (for example Skinner, 1954). In the linear type of programme the learning material is typically broken into small steps or frames. Information is presented in such a way that when a question is eventually asked, the correct answer is very likely to occur. The learner gets feedback on the response and proceeds to the next frame. Although errors can occur, they are kept to a minimum by the use of prompts, and by keeping the 'steps' as small as possible. In a linear programme every learner will see exactly the same sequence of frames, but the pace with which the programme is completed will be determined by individual differences.

Other programmes can show remedial frames if the answers are inadequate at various points in the programme and are called *branching* programmes (for example Crowder, 1960). Branching programmes typically contain more information per frame. The questions at the end of the frame are essentially diagnostic indicating whether the learner can proceed to absorb new information or whether remedial instruction is necessary. If an incorrect answer is given a number of alternative 'branches' are available to provide remedial instruction dependent upon the nature of the learner's mistake. Eventually the learner returns to the original learning route. For a discussion of the relative merits of linear, branching and other types of programme, the reader should refer to the books cited at the beginning of this section. The final items, (*d*), (*e*) and (*f*), are not controversial and are features of good training schemes irrespective of whether or not they are programmed.

The enduring contribution of programmed instruction to training has been to focus attention on the objectives of training programmes, and to close the teaching loop, by requiring responses from trainees and giving feedback to them in the light of these responses.

Computer assisted instruction
The power of modern computing facilities has now increased the technology available to programmed instruction. A large computer can be programmed with complex branching rules, and a large capacity exists for storing information. The student interacts with the computer via a 'terminal'. This is usually a teleprinter, but can be a visual display with a sophisticated input, such as a 'light' pen which enables direct communication with the display. The computer can be programmed to exert very flexible control over the learning situation, adopting different styles of presentation on the basis of the student's responses and stored data about him, e.g. previous intellectual performance. The student's interactions with the computer can be of an informal nature. The computer can greet the student and the

interaction can take the form of a conversation, the computer asking questions of the student and giving appropriate comments on his performance in everyday terms using encouraging or even admonitory phrases. The responses allowed by the system can range widely, as the computer can be programmed to accept misspellings, synonyms and words in the wrong order, etc.

The great flexibility of the computer in adapting to the student means that as well as the student learning the material, the computer also learns about student, adapting its behaviour to the demands of the learner in terms of instructional style etc. Developments in computer assisted instruction (CAI) have occurred both in America (Stolurow, 1967) and Britain (Seeman and Hartley, 1969). The high costs of CAI can be offset by economy of scale since a large computer can serve many student 'terminals' on a time-sharing basis.

Evaluation of programmed instruction

The basic problem of evaluating any type of programmed instruction is to decide with what alternative teaching method to compare it. In a classroom learning situation if a teacher is used at least four difficulties arise. The information is delivered aurally rather than visually, motivation may be affected by the novelty of using a programme, the amount of time spent learning is difficult to control and also the level of ability of the teacher is important. Notwithstanding these problems the efficiency (and therefore effectiveness) of programmed instruction has been evaluated. A number of reviews have confirmed the

Table 5.1 The results of 112 studies comparing programmed with conventional instructions (Hartley, 1972a)

Measures recorded	Number of studies recording these measures	Programmed Instruction Group		
		Significantly superior	Not significantly different	Significantly worse
Time taken	90	47	37	6
Test results	110	41	54	15
Retest results	33	6	24	3

Note: Figures in the first column differ because not all three measures are recorded for every one of the 112 studies.

general superiority of programmed instruction (e.g. Hartley, 1972a). In a review of evaluation, Hartley summarises the results of 112 studies which demonstrate superiority of programmed instruction in terms of time taken to learn, test and retest results (Table 5.1). However any exhaustive evaluation must include the additional criterion of cost benefit and Hartley presents examples of the estimated savings of industrial applications of programmed instruction (Table 5.2).

Table 5.2 The cost benefits of programmed instruction (Hartley, 1972a)

Investi-gations	Cost of Program	Cost of Conventional Instruction	Estimated Savings
1	—	—	20%–50% of training time
2	$218 per student hour	$309 per student hour	29% of instruction 27% of trainee time
3	—	—	$90,000 in training to date ($30/man.)
4	£1,500	£1,500	£1,500 per yr
5	£20,000	—	1 week's trainee time. Approx. £10,000 per yr
6	£12,500	—	8·2% of training time. £24,700 after 2 yrs
7	—	—	3 hrs. per supervisor. $90,000 per course
8	£550	—	£1,275 annually
9	£13,500	—	£1,000 for every 3 courses
10	—	—	10 weeks trainee time. Labour turnover reduced from 70% to 30%. Retention of skilled labour

Gagné's learning hierarchy

There are various methods of organizing material in a programmed fashion. Gagné's scheme is particularly important since it is theoretically based. The theory is one of instruction rather than learning. Gagné is more concerned with organization of the conditions for promoting learning than the mechanisms of learning. Gagné's ideas are probably best presented in his book entitled *The Conditions of Learning* (1970). His previous taxonomy of eight learning types could be used for classifying elements of job performance during a task analysis (see pp. 50–1). Gagné's taxonomy is not only a scheme for classifying behaviour but also has important implications for sequencing of information for training. The eight types of learning can be arranged hierarchically as in Fig. 5.3. This hierarchical structure is important, as it reveals the sequence in which task components should be learned. It can be seen that 'problem

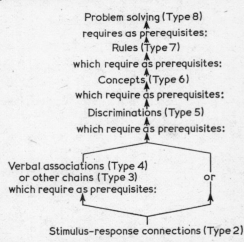

Fig. 5.3 *Gagné's (1970) learning hierarchy*

solving' requires as prerequisites that the 'rules' used for solving problems be learned which in turn require as prerequisites that the 'concepts' used in such rules are already mastered. Gagné's scheme therefore advocates that instruction should proceed from the lower to the higher levels of the learning hierarchy. It does not maintain that learning cannot occur without such sequences but merely that they provide the optimal way of arranging the conditions for learning.

Duncan (1972) points out that slight adjustments have been made to Gagné's scheme over a series of publications. The most important change being in the relative positions of 'discrimination' and 'chains' in the learning hierarchy. Fig. 5.3 is based on Gagné (1970) in which 'discrimination' occurs at a higher level than 'chains', whereas in an earlier version (Gagné's 1965)

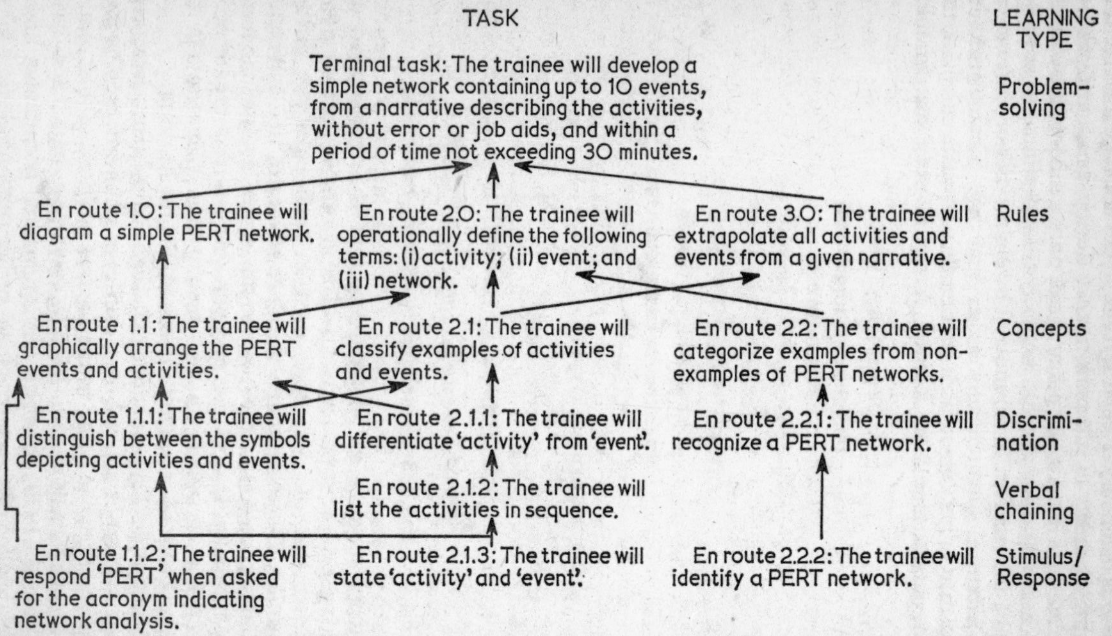

TASK

LEARNING TYPE

Terminal task: The trainee will develop a simple network containing up to 10 events, from a narrative describing the activities, without error or job aids, and within a period of time not exceeding 30 minutes.

Problem-solving

En route 1.0: The trainee will diagram a simple PERT network.

En route 2.0: The trainee will operationally define the following terms: (i) activity; (ii) event; and (iii) network.

En route 3.0: The trainee will extrapolate all activities and events from a given narrative.

Rules

En route 1.1: The trainee will graphically arrange the PERT events and activities.

En route 2.1: The trainee will classify examples of activities and events.

En route 2.2: The trainee will categorize examples from non-examples of PERT networks.

Concepts

En route 1.1.1: The trainee will distinguish between the symbols depicting activities and events.

En route 2.1.1: The trainee will differentiate 'activity' from 'event'.

En route 2.2.1: The trainee will recognize a PERT network.

Discrimination

En route 2.1.2: The trainee will list the activities in sequence.

En route 1.1.2: The trainee will respond 'PERT', when asked for the acronym indicating network analysis.

En route 2.1.3: The trainee will state 'activity' and 'event'.

En route 2.2.2: The trainee will identify a PERT network.

Verbal chaining

Stimulus/ Response

Fig. 5.4 *Learning hierarchy for constructing PERT networks (Adapted from Lawson, 1974)*

these positions are reversed. This is an important change in the light of a study by Duncan (1969). Two component tasks were isolated in an analysis of an acid purification process in the chemical industry which involved lengthy start-up and shut-down procedures. Fixed sequences of operations or chains were required involving the location and then manipulation of various controls in the plant complex. Duncan compared two groups of trainees. One was given pretraining on the necessary names and locations of the equipment (discriminations) before being trained on the sequence of operations (chains). The other group had no pretraining, starting directly with the sequence. The pretrained group performed faster, although there was no difference in error rates or subsequent retention after completion of training. This study suggests that there may be advantages to structuring the training material in a hierarchical manner. Interestingly, Duncan's example is consistent with the relative position of 'chains' and 'discrimination' in Gagné's earlier version but not with his later formulation. Despite this small ambiguity between these adjacent learning categories, the present authors nevertheless feel that the general approach warrants closer attention in the training area.

A recent industrial application is given by Lawson (1974) who considers task analysis, after Gagné, as important (Fig. 5.4). From the analysis it should be possible to identify the component learning tasks or what 'en route' learning is required to reach terminal performance. Lawson gives the example of a management problem solving task, the learning hierarchy of which is given in Fig. 5.4. The task is the construction of a PERT (Programme Evaluation and Review Technique) network, which is a procedure for planning projects. The activities and their sequences are analysed and diagrammed. Here we can see the different kinds of learning involved and the objectives of then 'en route' learning tasks. The order for training is to proceed upwards through the hierarchy.

Gagné's scheme therefore relates the two major functions in training of task analysis and training design. The training sequence is suggested by the types of learning, isolated during task analysis. There are various methods which may facilitate learning, from extrinsic feedback and guidance techniques described in Chapter 4, to programmed instruction.

Part and whole training

Recent work in task analysis has stressed determining the nature and interrelations of operations involved in a task. If a task can be broken down to a greater or lesser extent into operations and suboperations, then what is the optimal method of practising these components which will lead to acceptable performance of the whole task? If parts are practised, how should they be reassembled into performance of the whole task? If a part training method is adopted, an additional problem is selecting from the range of part methods, the main variants of which are:

Pure part. Parts are learned to some criterion, or for a fixed number of trials in isolation. They are then combined in whole task practice. Two variations of this are the Repetitive practice condition (not the repetitive 'part' method given below) where individual parts are practised repeatedly and the Consecutive condition where the parts, though practised in isolation, follow the sequence of the whole task.

Progressive part. The first and second parts are practised in isolation, then they are practised together. A third part can then be practised in isolation and then combined with parts one and two. Any subsequent parts are also practised in isolation and then added to those already combined.

Repetitive part. The first part is practised in isolation and then combined with the second part. The third is then added to the practice unit. Successive parts are added in the same way.

Retrogressive part. This is sometimes called the reversed repetitive method. As its name implies it involves practice of the last part in isolation, then the last and the penultimate, thus leading up to practice of the whole task by adding parts in the reverse order.

Isolated part. In this technique, some parts of the task are practised on their own, before whole task practice.

The part/whole question then is a nice example of the kind of practical problem a technology of training should be able to answer. Examination of the extensive literature of part versus

84

whole training reveals a conspicuous absence of consistent results favouring one method (e.g. Naylor, 1962). Therefore traditionally a recommendation has been that whole methods should be initially implemented with part methods reserved in case difficulties should arise. On the other hand part methods have found favour in industry and a number of popular texts and training board publications recommend them. There are well documented cases where progressive-part methods have been very successful (Seymour, 1966). An emphasis on part methods for manual repetitive industrial tasks has led to their inappropriate use, and there have been recent comments on this in the clothing industry in both America (Victor, 1971) and Britain (Toye, 1969). The former paper is a general attack on 'analytic' or part methods of training, and although little data are presented, Victor suggests that a technique of successive approximations of the whole task is a more efficient approach. Toye (1969) outlines the advantages of carefully designed 'basic skills' exercises but adds the proviso 'use a whole sequence of task operations to avoid isolating the skill elements from their context and so distorting them'. Here, he appears to heed the warning of Crossman (1959) who, in the context of his theory of skill learning, talks of a learner 'selecting' response patterns from his repertoire. In training it is necessary to select the 'right' response patterns, the 'wrong' ones being those 'that are optimum in the isolated element but not in the complete task'. These conflicting recommendations may be a consequence of different task characteristics being confounded.

Any particular task will have its own characteristics which may determine the more efficient training method. What is required is the establishment of a set of rules or principles of training relating task characteristics to training methods. The process of task analysis and training design would be simpler if such principles existed.

Task characteristics and training principles
The obvious first step is to scrutinise the task in question in terms of the demands which various task characteristics will place upon the trainee's information processing capacities. The learning demands of the components and their interrelations should be specified in informational terms which are then relevant to training rather than using such ambiguous terms as 'difficulty'. Two groups of workers, Naylor and Briggs (1963)

and Annett and Kay (1956), have sought such solutions to the part/whole problem by proposing certain training principles which will be more closely examined.

The 1963 paper of Naylor and Briggs is the best exposition of the 'Naylor Hypothesis' which details the characteristics of a task determining the relative efficiency of whole or part training. The hypothesis elaborates two task characteristics of 'organization' and 'complexity' as important. Task organization 'refers to the demands imposed on the subject due to the nature of the interrelationship existing among the several task dimensions'. Interrelatedness of task components occurs when information displayed in one task component is relevant to another. Task complexity is determined by 'the demands placed on subject's information processing and/or memory storage capacities by each of the task dimensions [components] separately'. These two parameters are viewed as combining multiplicately to determine the learning difficulty of the task and the hypothesis itself is comprised of the following two principles:

Principle 1: Given a task of relatively high organization, as task complexity is increased whole task training should become relatively more efficient than the part task methods.
Principle 2: Given a task of relatively low organization, an increase in task complexity should result in part methods becoming relatively superior to whole task training. (Blum and Naylor, 1968: 248)

This hypothesis has been partially substantiated by two experiments (Briggs *et al.*, 1962) although the only decisive test and confirmation is provided by one experiment (Naylor and Briggs, 1963). Further indirect evidence is provided by a number of studies of perceptual-motor skill. Coordinated perceptual-motor activity was required in studies of complex level positioning, tracking, simulated aircraft manoeuvre and controlling a guided missile simulator. Presumably these tasks are highly 'organized', in Naylor's terms, because of the interacting informational demands of the task components. Whole training was found superior to part training in all the above studies which is consistent with the first principle of Naylor's hypothesis.

A major difficulty in applying this hypothesis is in specifying, for any particular task, the levels of complexity and organization. Also it has not been applied to tasks involving long sequences or 'chains' of operations, for example assembly tasks or sequences of switching operations. Sheffield (1961) proposed that part methods are more appropriate for such tasks but the evidence is equivocal.

Annett and Kay (1956) examine learning from the trainee's perspective and propose a very different principle to guide the selection of part or whole training. They suggest that skill acquisition can be conceptualized as a change in the informational value of signals during the course of learning. In any task, stimuli can be viewed as a series of more or less predictable events. Predictability depends upon the variability of the series and the extent to which it has been learned. Tasks may be categorized as to whether or not the subject's responses influence the nature of subsequent signals from a display. When they do not influence the display (i.e. task elements are independent) and the person simply has to learn the characteristics of the signal sequence, whole training is often more appropriate. When responses do influence the display (i.e. task elements are interdependent), adequate responses will mask the true nature of subsequent signals, making the series difficult to learn. In this situation, part training will be superior by facilitating response consistency which will produce more predictable signal sequences. The Annett and Kay 'principle' can be summarised as follows:

if the elements of a task are highly independent the task is best learned as a whole, but where elements are highly interdependent, they should be split up and the task learned in parts. (1956: 114)

This principle contradicts the Naylor hypothesis because if 'highly interdependent' is equated with 'high organization', Naylor's advice is whole training whilst Annett and Kay's is part training. This contradiction stems from emphasizing different aspects of the task. Naylor adopts an engineering point of view where 'high organization' refers to the potential of information from one task component facilitating performance of another. Annett and Kay's interdependence is operator orientated and refers to the possibility of such facilitation not being achieved because inadequate responses will disrupt the information flow.

These two principles can be seen as complementary, however, since both Naylor's system-based and Annett and Kay's operator-based viewpoints are important in any particular situation. Questions must be asked about organization and complexity (Naylor) and interdependence (Annett and Kay) to determine the more appropriate training method. A decision tree for such a purpose is represented in Fig. 5.5.

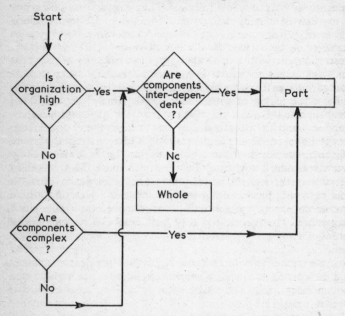

Fig. 5.5 *A decision tree for selecting part or whole training methods*

Future research should be directed at assessing the usefulness of the above principles in resolving the part versus whole controversy.

Massed versus distributed training

Up to now in this chapter, the temporal distribution of the presentation of information has been ignored. But, is it better to have training sessions close together or spaced? This refers to a classical and well documented debate in psychology, of the relative efficiency of massed versus distributed practice. (see A3) The fact that Welford (1968), in consideration of the optimum length of a training session, adds very little new evidence to that presented in the early fifties, suggests that the principles for deciding between massed and distributed training are fairly well established. There is some confusion in this area as to what is actually distributed. The interval between training sessions may vary, the sessions themselves may vary in duration or both may change simultaneously. In the former, most common situation, further problems concern whether or not to exclude the periods between practice sessions in evaluation of the efficiency of massed and distributed training. Typically, studies have adopted a theoretical approach, ignoring the 'total-time' in training, and found that distributed training is generally superior; if the practically important variable of the time between sessions is included, massed training is inevitably more efficient. Another problem is whether differences between these two conditions of training really reflect underlying levels of *learning* as distinguished from temporary *performance* levels, an important difference mentioned in Chapter 2. Massed training produces a sort of 'psychological fatigue' (Holding, 1965) which may inhibit the manifestation of true levels of learning. As a consequence, a massed training procedure will *show* an improvement *between* sessions rather than *within* sessions as it allows time for such inhibition to dissipate. On changing from massed to a distributed schedule, performance improves so rapidly that the previous level of learning must have been masked during massed training. Ammons (1947) shows that performance efficiency may rise from 18 to 43 per cent if a rest of 5–20 minutes follows an 8 minute continuous work period. The claimed superiority of distributed training must be tempered in the light of these results.

The relative efficiency of these training schedules will depend upon the demands of the following factors associated with the task:

(a) *Memory:* If the rest periods are too long, then forgetting may occur with the subsequent need for relearning. On the other hand, such intervals may allow the trainee to rehearse (covertly or overtly) and therefore consolidate memory traces (Welford, 1968).The opportunity for rehearsal may, however, be limited by performance of a task in between practice sessions, and original learning impaired, depending on the degree of similarity of the tasks. A complicating factor is that rest periods may facilitate the forgetting of incorrect responses.

(b) *Warm-up:* After a rest period the trainee will have to reacclimatize and reorient himself to the task which may take some time. This suggests that the rest period should not be too long.

(c) *'Psychological fatigue':* If rest periods are too short, then the trainee may suffer from possible inhibitory carry-over effects from previous learning which is characteristic of some perceptual-motor tasks as mentioned above. This detrimental effect is in practice difficult to differentiate from increasing fatigue and a loss of motivation. Both of these will also increase with more massing of training.

It is difficult to give universal guidelines on selecting the more efficient training schedule. It will depend upon the nature of the specific task demands. Generally some form of distributed practice appears desirable for both verbal and perceptual-motor tasks, although the optimal duration of the rest interval will depend upon how important memory, warm-up and 'psychological fatigue' are to any specific task.

6
Simulation for training

In our discussion of sequencing of information for training we mentioned that simple instructions and demonstrations would sometimes provide sufficient training, whilst for complex and/or critical tasks, more attention need be given. Related to this issue is the decision as to where the training should be administered. There is a dichotomy between training administered 'on-the-job', i.e. in the normal work situation, and training given 'off-the-job', i.e. outside the work situation. Training in the latter sense involves some form of simulation. Gagné (1962b) has detailed three important features of any simulators for training:

(a) a simulator attempts to *represent* a real situation in which operations are carried out;
(b) a simulator provides its users with certain *controls* over that situation;
(c) the simulator is deliberately designed to *omit* certain parts of the real operational situation.

The principle guiding the degree of representation of the real situation together with the omission of certain parts is that aspects of the task should be selected relevant to the training purpose. Therefore simulation for training will seek to represent task demands rather than mimicking the material situation. As a consequence, training simulators may range from paper flow-diagrams and cardboard models to computer controlled equipment.

The operational situation is often not the best place in which to learn to perform the task. This may be due to the nature of human learning, and/or the characteristics of the task and its context.

Costs and consequences of error. The early stages of learning are characterized by errors which would be intolerable for training in some job situations, such as learning to fly where errors may be costly both in human and hardware terms. Johnson (1968) reports that 'during the twenty-four months prior to June 1967 airlines lost eight jets and twenty-six crew members during training flights.' Even with less complex tasks, costs of error may be high. One faulty item in a production process may not be expensive, but under large scale production, costs of error may become an important factor. Simulators can be used to reduce these costs.

Provision of extra information. Simulators provide an environment in which errors or poor performance can be allowed, and where it is possible to give appropriate feedback to the trainee. The simulator can thus give extrinsic feedback, or guidance. It may not be possible to actually measure performance and give feedback 'on-the-job', but simulation can be designed to incorporate this information, essential for efficient learning. In this case the simulator has additional features not present in the real situation.

Removing environmental stressors. Another feature of the 'on-the-job' situation is that the task may be performed in an environment not conducive to learning, e.g., in noise, heat, or vibration. The learning environment should be examined from an ergonomics point of view. One solution is to provide some form of 'sheltered' simulator position, near the work situation, which will reduce environmental stressors for the trainee.

Manipulation of temporal dimensions. In simulation the ability to manipulate the time dimensions of the task may have considerable advantages. For example, some start-up or shut-down procedures in the petrochemical industries take a long time because of the slow response characteristics of the plant. This means the learner is confronted with unnecessarily long periods of inactivity between responses, coupled with the infrequent occurrence of these tasks anyway. Simulation permits practice of more instances of the task than possible on-the-job, and without long periods of inactivity between task components. Another reason for distorting temporal characteristics of tasks is to increase experience of rare emergencies and faults. Hopefully, with any well-designed system such contingencies should be infrequent but when performance is required it needs to be executed at a high level of proficiency, thus experience of all the possible faulty states may take a long time. Simulation of such faulty conditions has been called 'collapsed experience', and is not only essential for the new trainee but is also useful to experienced personnel in the form of refresher courses.

Part-task simulation. Part-task simulators can provide training for any number of the task components. For example, 'procedure trainers' used in flight training neglect display-control interactions and isolate the procedural aspects which can be practised separately. Part-task simulators can therefore be relatively economic and simple devices if used for only the necessary task components, although some whole-task practice will usually be necessary as well. The amount of whole-task practice need only be short on occasions. For example, Adams and Hufford (1962) compared whole or part learning for a simulated aircraft manoeuvre. The performance of the part group whilst inferior on the first attempt of whole task practice was equivalent to that of the whole group on the second attempt. Sometimes a progression from part to whole task simulators is feasible and more economic than the use of only whole-task simulators.

Lower running costs. As we shall see later in this chapter, cost is an important factor influencing the use of simulators. One advantage is that the running costs of a simulator may be lower than those of operational equipment. Johnson (1968) estimates the operating costs of a Trident aircraft simulator as approximately one-fourteenth of that of the actual aircraft. This is not necessarily always true, and it is possible to envisage some simulators costing more to run than real equipment, although the essential consideration is their cost-effectiveness for training.

Inaccessibility of tasks for training. This is manifested in two ways. Firstly, some tasks may not exist operationally, for example, in industry, training before commissioning of a new plant is important. Secondly, the environment of other tasks may preclude opportunities for practice. An extreme example is training astronauts for a moon landing, where training could hardly be given in the real situation!

Varieties of simulation

The following discussion does not claim to be exhaustive, but attempts to indicate that a wide range of simulations exist. What is simulated might be the equipment, the material, or situations which provoke categories of behaviour, or any combination of these.

A number of reviews of simulators for training are available (e.g. Gagné, 1962b) and a recent issue of *Human Factors* 1973, *15* (6), covers the area of aircraft simulators in detail. The development of aircraft simulators is a leading area in *equipment* simulation and has produced many ideas of general relevance to other areas of training, especially those involving some form of vehicular control, e.g. trains, ships, and cars. Simulation for driving training is an interesting case. Many people are engaged in learning this high level skill, although unlike many other areas of training for personal rather than vocational reasons. Several different car simulators exist. Some are simple representations of the car's displays and controls, with films being shown of traffic situations. Others use real cars, or parts of them, and are more dynamic because the operations performed by the driver result in changes in the visual field. This is achieved by, in one example, the moving of a television camera over a stationary terrain model. The responses of the driver bring about appropriate proportional changes in the rate and direction of camera movements. The picture displayed thus behaves in a realistic way when controls are used (see Schori, 1970, for fuller descriptions of car simulators). Surprisingly, these methods have not gained wide acceptance in the driving schools, despite their potential contributions. A study by the Road Research Laboratory has however shown no great advantages in terms of learning for a particular car simulator over normal car training (Henry,

1973). More research is obviously needed in this area. If it is demonstrated that simulators are as good as cars for early training their usefulness can be evaluated in terms of relative costs.

Other training devices simulate the *material* being worked upon. Examples can be found in dentistry and with tasks involving sewing machines. Dental students can utilize 'phantom heads' for practising drilling teeth, which has obvious advantages during early training. For some years in the clothing industry, paper or other cheap material has been substituted for cloth in training the basic skills for sewing. Toye (1969) warns that, although this uses cheap material, it may inhibit acquisition of the appropriate skills for guiding cloth through the machine, because characteristics of the material are very different from those in the real task. He recommends the use of fabric closer in characteristics to the actual material to be used.

Let us now consider the simulations of *behavioural* components of situations. One example is the simulation of person-to-person interactions. Many service industries are concerned with such interactions. The distributive, hotel and catering, air transport and travel industries all have tasks of this kind, e.g. sales transactions, waitering. The skills involved here are termed 'customer contact skills' (Nixon, 1974, provides a useful review of this area). One method of simulation is to ask trainees to 'role-play', which involves playing the part of a job incumbent, e.g. hotel receptionist. The trainer, or another trainee, plays the role of 'customer'. They act out a situation which can be video-taped and replayed, with suitable comment and suggestions from the trainer.

Another approach to consider is the simulation training of decision making using hypothetical problems. In management training 'business games' are sometimes used. The persons under training again play a role, are given particular goals to achieve and resources to deploy. Performance is assessed in an individual or competitive situation. In these two examples, simulation is no longer equipment or material based. These types of simulation have some aspects in common, however. The trainee familiarizes himself with representations of different stimulus situations, makes responses, and can receive appropriate feedback.

A somewhat novel variety of simulation is suggested by

Prather (1973). He considers that mental imagery can aid training by simulating tasks through the use of thought processes. Trainee pilots were played tapes which prompted 'mental' practice of manoeuvres for landing aircraft whilst they sat in simulated cockpits, not overtly performing. When subsequently compared with trainees who did not have this practice, they were rated better in their landing skill proficiency.

Fidelity of simulation

Fidelity of simulation usually refers to the degree of realism or the degree of representation of the real task by the simulator. Any training device is used with the underlying assumption that on changing from the simulated to the real situation, the trainee will perform at an acceptable level. Therefore, as well as a physical transfer from the training situation to the job, we are also concerned with the 'transfer' of learning, which:

> occurs whenever the existence of a previously established habit or *skill* has an influence upon the acquisition, performance or relearning of another habit or *skill*. 'Positive transfer' occurs when the existence of the previous habit or *skill* facilitates learning the new one; 'negative transfer' refers to the interference by a previously learned habit or *skill* on new learning. (*Glossary of Training Terms*, 1971).

General principles have been derived from many psychological experiments which help the trainer to predict whether transfer of training is likely to be positive or negative. These principles, summarised by Holding (1965) and Ellis (1965), are by no means uncomplicated and can only be applied by close analysis of the similarity between the original and transfer task, the conditions and level of training and the ability of the trainee. Laboratory studies have varied the degree of response and stimulus similarity between the original and transfer tasks although in complex interactive tasks this may be misleading with both changing simultaneously. Nevertheless the following two principles serve as useful guidelines to the trainer:

Stimulus similarity
When a task requires the learner to make the same response

to new but similar stimuli, positive transfer increases with increasing stimulus similarity.

Response similarity
When a task requires the learner to make a new or different response to the same stimuli, transfer tends to be negative and increases as the responses become less similar.

(a) Under conditions of high response similarity, this condition can produce positive transfer.
(b) Also, it is usually more difficult under this condition to obtain negative transfer in verbal learning than it is in motor skills learning.

(Ellis, 1965: 73)

It is therefore important that when using any simulator, the stimulus and response components should be analysed and represented in the light of their potential transfer effects.

In attempts to maximize positive transfer of learning, simulators have often been built which have a high fidelity. Degree of fidelity is usually viewed as an increasing positive function of the degree of representation of the task components in terms of the equipment, material and behavioural situations mentioned in the previous section. Increasing degree of fidelity usually implies increasing cost of simulation. It has been previously stressed that in the efficient design of training, terminal performance criteria should be specified. The resources available for training should also be known. With both the knowledge of terminal performance and the limits of resources, the designer of a training system must then decide upon the nature and extent of simulation training. A hypothetical relationship between transfer of training, cost of simulation and degree of fidelity has been suggested by R. B. Miller (1954) and is presented in Fig. 6.1. It should be stressed that these curves are hypothetical and are based on experience in the training area rather than experimental evidence. It suggests that costs of simulation can rise particularly steeply with any small increases associated in the higher degree of fidelity range. On the other hand, the transfer of training function rises fairly steeply with increasing fidelity and then levels off. Where the curves are furthest apart is designated 'the point of diminishing returns' and represents the highest transfer to cost ratio. Further investment in simulation produces smaller associated increases in transfer. These decisions in real training situations will depend upon the extent to which less than perfect terminal performance is tolerable. For some tasks perfect transfer is necessary, whilst for others less than perfect can be acceptable. A pragmatic approach would be to develop simulators with increasing degrees of fidelity, until either acceptable levels of performance are reached or unacceptable costs are approached, at which stage the training system designer must refer the problem to higher authority.

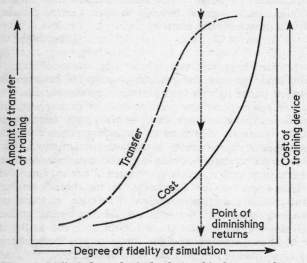

Fig. 6.1 *Miller's hypothetical relationship between degree of simulator fidelity, transfer, training and cost of simulator* (*Adapted from Biel, 1962: 374*)

Hammerton (1967) reviews the range of measures of transfer of training relevant to simulators. There are basically two categories. The first concerns the amount of time of training saved by simulation relative to normal training ('savings' measures) and the second concerns the initial scores on transfer to the real situation ('first-shot' measures). The evaluation of any particular simulator will not necessarily be the same from these two indices, and their validity will depend upon the training programme objectives. If first-shot performance is important, then high fidelity is an advantage. If this is not necessary then a lower fidelity simulator producing a reasonable saving score may yield acceptably rapid learning on transfer. Studies by Hammerton (1966) showed that a range of visual fidelity in a simulator produced a fairly constant and high savings score, but a range of from good to bad first-shot measures of transfer.

Quite high levels of transfer can be found from quite low fidelity simulators. In a study of training of US Army personnel for operating a 92-step procedure on a control panel, Cox *et al* (1965) compared a range of simulators. These varied from the real equipment, valued at $11,000, a high fidelity simulator ($3,000), a lower fidelity panel in which the displays and controls did not move ($1,000), cheap cardboard models, photographs, to finally a reduced size drawing. Different groups were trained with these devices and were equivalent in terms of training time, post-training test and retention. Thus the same amounts of transfer were obtained despite decreasing degrees of fidelity. A possible explanation is that all of these simulations included the critical task features necessary for learning and therefore the degree of representation equipment-wise was irrelevant. Therefore emphasis in simulator design should be to achieve the most appropriate and economic conditions for learning rather than a high fidelity of simulation per se. Thus there should be a close relationship between task analysis demands and their training requirements and the design of simulators. In this way simulation becomes part of the overall training design process, and consideration should be given to the full range of fidelity of simulation and the potential for presenting task relevant features. Ideas about skill learning (see Chs. 2, 4 and 5) should influence simulator design, which has been remarked upon by Jamieson (1973). Close examination of the skill to be learned should reveal the essential features to be incorporated in any simulator, e.g. perceptual cues both for input and feedback. The theoretical background of skill acquisition might also dictate that certain *extra* features should be included in any simulation, e.g. extrinsic feedback. Interestingly this means that transfer from a training device with extra features has the possibility of being higher than that from the real situation.

There are of course other training media and devices available for training besides simulators. Biel (1962) presents the following list of 'training aids' which includes some of the types of simulators described above:

Wall charts
Transparencies and slides
Films
Closed-circuit TV
Teaching machines.

Again each medium of information presentation should be judged on its efficiency and relevance for the task in question. Training should concentrate on the relevant task demands and presentation of information may be more efficient by one 'aid' rather than another. Research in this area has been discussed by Lumsdaine (1962).

Conclusion

Simulation exists in many forms and is attractive for a variety of reasons. It offers the potential for improved efficiency in training for a large range of tasks. It should not be forgotten, however, that one component of the real task will usually be missing, i.e. stress of the real situation, unless deception is employed. The real stress of threat to life or limb, or control of large capital investment, is difficult to simulate satisfactorily, if only for ethical reasons. Therefore, it should not be thought that training ends with transfer to the job situation. No matter how high the level of fidelity of simulation, it should, where possible, be followed by some on-the-job training or supervision.

7
Individual differences

Up to now the heterogeneity of the trainee population has been ignored. A general information processing model of human performance has been presented and the general efficiency of different methods, of promoting learning of the task features, derived from task analysis, has been discussed. However, these generalizations refer to the average of a collection of varying scores derived from a sample of people. Some people will be better than average at some tasks and inferior at others. Whilst the training programme may use the optimal method of presenting the task information to the average trainee, a range of characteristics of the trainee may determine its effectiveness and efficiency. Some of these differences in characteristics will have such an influence on the success of the programmes that the trainer must be aware of them. Ideally then, the training programme should be able to accommodate the individual differences of the trainee. In terms of the informational model of skill, individual differences may occur at any of the stages between input and translation to output, i.e. perception, short or long-term memory, choice of action or control of the motor output. On the other hand important individual differences may occur in the energy necessary to power such a system in terms of the trainee's attitudes or level of motivation. The importance of these individual differences will of course depend upon the nature of the tasks to be mastered. Training necessarily interacts with the process of selection, hence people with serious visual defects will be automatically excluded from any training scheme for pilots. At the other extreme, psychology has demonstrated that many individuals labelled 'retarded', 'disadvantaged' or 'handicapped' in physical or mental terms and 'rejected' by society, particularly by employers, can be trained to perform a wide variety of tasks at a normal level of competency. The importance of individual differences will also vary with the stage of training, hence a person of low verbal ability may find it initially difficult to absorb verbal instructions of how to operate a machine which would enable him to develop an appropriate 'plan' of action. Alternatively, as will be discussed later, an older trainee may be limited in speed of responding which may only become manifest late in training. Firstly the notion of ability patterns will be examined and then the effect of age, intelligence, and personality of the trainee.

The concept of abilities

Psychologists generally view individual differences in performance and learning as reflecting underlying differences in motor and mental ability. Some abilities are general, pervading performance of many varied tasks, whilst others are task specific. Therefore in the ideal situation these abilities would be assessed and matched to the abilities required to perform a task and training would be minimal as a consequence. Unfortunately such an ideal has not yet been reached and has often resulted in the popular misconception that some people are untrainable.

Firstly let us examine the notion of an ability with reference to some insightful comments by Ferguson (1954) who relates the concepts of learning, transfer of learning and ability. An ability can be operationally defined in terms of what a person can do. Yet learning or training experiments are concerned in a sense with changes in 'ability' to perform certain tasks although the word is not normally used here. Its usage is typically restricted to relatively non-fluctuating performance on standard tests. Ferguson suggests that an ability is really a manifestation of a previously overlearned pattern of behaviour which has reached the limit of improvement. Hence in learning situations the notion of abilities being important really refers to the fact that some prior overlearned pattern of behaviour may transfer positively or negatively to the new situation. Hence in learning we are actually concerned with the transfer of previously learned skills. The original development of any skill will depend upon cultural, environmental and biological factors. Cultural and environmental demands and opportunities will differ between societies and for each individual within a society. For example, in our society there is an emphasis upon speed and accuracy of verbal performance which is therefore reflected in the construction of intelligence tests. However, the conclusion from an intelligence or any other type of test that performance is a reflection of an ability and is therefore unalterable is not necessarily true. Environmental demand or opportunity may have limited the development of the ability which may have been manifested under conditions of learning and overlearning.

Motor ability

In the area of physical education research, a great amount of effort has been directed at determining whether a general ability or many specific abilities affect success in various sports. The existence of such 'abilities' is inferred from correlations between performance of different tasks. It is assumed that a high positive correlation between performance of two tasks indicates an underlying common factor. Such an approach has not been particularly successful in sports psychology and generally each task has a fairly unique pattern of different abilities. This is hardly surprising if one remembers from Chapter 2 that there were many different aspects of even proprioceptive ability which were independent.

The work of Fleishman and his associates (e.g. Fleishman, 1966) adopted a correlational approach and was influenced by Ferguson's ideas. From an examination of many tasks administered to thousands of subjects different abilities were postulated to explain the common statistical variation between performance of the tasks.

These included such abilities as 'multilimb co-ordination', 'control precision' and 'manual dexterity', the importance of which will depend not only upon the nature of the task but also upon its stage of learning. Fig. 7.1 shows how the importance of various factors changes over practice sessions for a visual discrimination reaction time task with the characteristic increase of a specific task factor. Verbal and spatial relations factors are decreasingly important with acquisition of the skill and groups stratified by tests measuring these factors confirm this (Fleishman and Hempel, 1955).

Fleishman and Rich (1963) examined learning a two-hand co-ordination task in which a 'target' had to be tracked by manipulation of two handles which affected movement of the target follower in the horizontal and vertical directions. Fig. 7.2 shows the performance of groups varying in spatial and proprioceptive sensitivity over ten practice sessions. The group high in spatial ability was superior to a low spatial ability group in the early stages of practice although this superiority disappeared later in practice. Conversely whilst performance did not differ between groups of high and low proprioceptive sensitivity early in practice, there was a gradual divergence in favour of the high

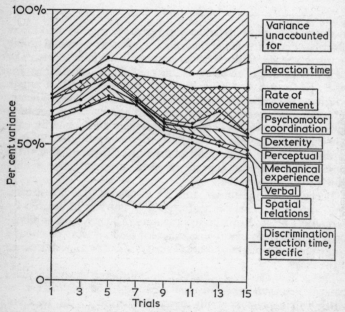

Fig. 7.1 *Percentage of variance represented by each factor at different stages of practice on the Discrimination Reaction Time Task. (Percentage of variance is represented by the area shaded in for each factor) (After Fleishman and Hempel, 1955)*

104

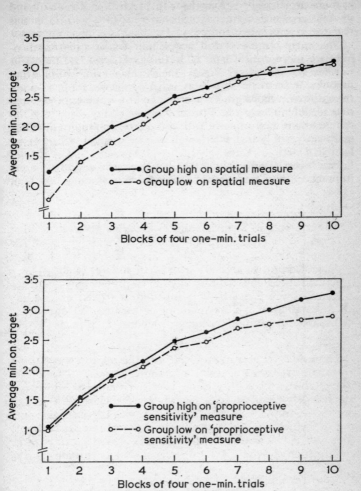

Fig. 7.2 *Comparison of Two-Hand Coordination acquisition curves for groups high and low on spatial ability and proprioceptive sensitivity. Data from Fleishman and Rich (1963)*

proprioceptive ability group later in practice. Such oft quoted findings are encouragingly consistent with Fitts' (1951) notion that the exteroceptive sources of feedback are more important in the early stages of skill acquisition whilst proprioceptive ones are more critical later in learning. At least two points of caution are necessary. Firstly Fleishman's criterion of what he called 'kinesthetic' sensitivity involved the discrimination between lifted weights which is only one of a number of possible tests of different aspects of proprioceptive ability. Secondly, the differences in performance within the levels of ability does not necessarily imply that this was due to differential utilization of feedback cues.

Fleishman (1968) claims that his approach is useful in the training setting, and quotes studies demonstrating this. For example, in citing an experiment by Fleishman and Fruchter (1960) he states:

we were able to identify abilities underlying the acquisition of skill at different stages of Morse Code learning, in an Air Force radio telegraphy school. Specifically, early learning depended on two auditory-perceptual abilities (auditory perceptual speed and auditory rhythm discrimination) and later learning was increasingly a function of 'speed of closure', representing an ability to unify or organise an apparently disparate field into meaningful units. (Fleishman, 1968: 183)

There are a number of problems with this approach, e.g. using an exhaustive range of tasks, labelling the statistical factors in meaningful psychological terms, and devising tests which unambiguously measure such factors. Nevertheless such an approach may provide information on changing task demands over practice which is useful in the design of any training programme (but also as information to the trainees). It also provides some confirmation of Fitts' (1962) notions of skill acquisition.

Intelligence and ability

A great deal of confusion stems from the simple usage of the word 'intelligence' as there is no specific activity which defines what is a polymorphous concept. There are many ways of being more or less intelligent. An operational definition of intelligence refers to what IQ tests measure, which includes vocabulary, memory, reasoning, etc. Most of these tests have time constraints which led Furneaux (1960) to argue that speed is the greatest facet of measured intelligence. The use of IQ tests as indicators of individuals' potential training problems will largely depend upon the demands of a particular task in terms of the speed and nature of the cognitive activities involved. The fact that some trainees may not have high levels of these relevant characteristics does not necessarily indicate that they are untrainable but that special provisions in the training programme may be able to compensate for these shortcomings.

Clarke (1966) summarizes the findings of a number of studies designed to evaluate the trainability and employability of adult imbeciles (IQ, 20–50). The conclusions are clear, that any conventional 'rejection' of such imbeciles on the basis of low IQ is wasteful since, with special training programmes, they can acquire and maintain simple perceptual-motor skills at the same level as those with considerably higher IQ. One study by Clarke and Hermelin (1955) showed that imbeciles could be taught tasks such as bicycle pump assembly, cutting insulated wire to an exact length and soldering four coloured wires to an eight pin television plug. Characteristically initial performance was very slow and inaccurate but although training takes longer, it was nevertheless effective eventually. Other similar investigations have corroborated this finding and also shown that retention and transfer of training can take place even with such low IQ groups, given a suitable training programme. Clarke (1966) proposes the following eight principles when training adult imbeciles for industrial work:

(a) The use of incentives.
(b) Task components taught separately but in the correct sequence.
(c) Ensuring the correct movements early in training.
(d) Distributed training.
(e) Overtraining.
(f) Verbalization during training.
(g) Emphasis on accuracy rather than speed early in training.
(h) Clear arrangement of material.

Gropper (1968) found differences in IQ related to training methods in an electric motor assembly task. Training method was varied with respect to how much of a procedural task was viewed in a demonstration before practice. As the length of the demonstration unit increased, performance of the low IQ group became less accurate unlike that of the high IQ group.

In a complex fault-finding task, Duncan (1971) found differences in transfer and retention between subjects of high and low ability. Ability was measured in terms of how well they searched for faults in some examples before training. Subjects were trained on a search task. After training, transfer was tested on another search task involving similar rules and retention of the original task, after three intervals ranging from immediately to six months. Ability was related to the amount of transfer of training with the high ability group superior at all three time intervals after training. However whilst high and low ability groups did not differ in immediate retention of the original task, differences emerged in favour of the high ability groups after the longer retention intervals. Duncan interprets this as evidence that the high ability group learned the general principles guiding search strategy whilst the low ability group learned the specific plan of the training task and therefore showed poor transfer and decreasing retention.

Ability will obviously determine the rate of acquisition of a task during training which makes it desirable to adapt the programme to the ability of each individual. This is obviously one of the advantages of programmed and computer assisted instruction techniques which can be adaptable and present the optimal level of difficulty of training material to each trainee besides allowing him to proceed at his preferred pace. In an unstructured situation where there are alternative courses of action open to the trainee, the less able may be more easily distracted by irrelevant information leading to an inefficient strategy (e.g. Dale, 1958). This would suggest that guidance training would be initially beneficial for such trainees.

Age

Rapid technological progress has resulted in changes in the type of job which a trainee must master and in the future possibly, economic considerations may lead to the mass running down of sections of industry in favour of more profitable ones. Both factors exacerbate the problems of retraining which are particularly acute for the older worker. The problems of the older worker have been the subject of a long-term research programme by Belbin and her associates (Belbin, 1964; Newsham 1969; Belbin and Belbin 1972). Firstly let us examine the different characteristics of the older worker which may be relevant to the problem of training before seeing how training programmes can accommodate them. Ironically, we will be making generalisations about individual differences, which do not apply to every older individual.

The characteristics, and particularly limitations, of the older person, have been well documented (Talland, 1968), and may be attributed to a decrease in the speed with which the central nervous system processes information (Birren, 1974), although this is far from certain. Physical abilities decline less with age than mental capacity which is consistent with statistical surveys reported by Murrell (1962) that the average age of labourers and packers is over 50 whilst disproportionately less old people are engaged in work which makes heavy 'perceptual' demands. There are a number of agreed limitations in the older person's information processing capacity of which the designer of any training programme should be aware. Crossman and Szafran (1956) found that older subjects discriminating cards or weights took longer as the number of alternatives and therefore their information content increased. Older people also find it more difficult to obliterate or ignore irrelevant features of the task (Rabbitt, 1965) and also people over 55 find it difficult to adapt to task information presented in a novel way, such as by a mirror (Welford, 1958). Furthermore there is an impairment in short-term memory as illustrated in Fig. 7.3 by an experiment by Talland (1968) in which subjects between 77 and 89 years remembered less than half the number of items of a 20–25 year old group in an immediate recall task. All of these impairments tend to inhibit progress in learning, particularly problem solving situations, and partly account for the characteristic 'slowing of responding' of the older person in more difficult tasks (Welford, 1958). In paced tasks older people perform less well and will also be more likely to adopt a preference for accuracy rather than speed which may be partly a compensatory strategy. Belbin and Belbin (1972) describe training 50-year-old Mrs Chatton in high speed sewing machine skills whereby 'at every stage she showed a disposition to pause for extra checks and inspections'. On the other hand when errors occur early in learning they tend to persist and the older person finds it difficult to eliminate them.

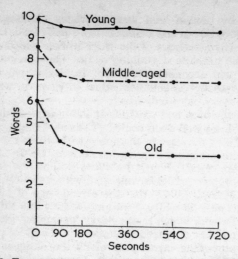

Fig. 7.3 *Forgetting curves of meaningful 3 letter words in repeated recall. Young men (N=20), aged 20–25; middle-aged men and women (N=40), aged 47–62 (mean 58); old men (N=20), aged 77–89 (mean 81) (Talland, 1968)*

Past experience may give advantages or disadvantages to the older worker. Previously learned specific skills will affect the degree to which new ones can be mastered. Also the development of a general line of attack for attempting to solve problems may be facilitated by 'learning how to learn' or hindered by a rigid and non-adaptive strategy. Attitudes of and concerning the older worker are also important. Generally the old person is less risky in decision making than the young. This may be allied to the observed reluctance of older workers to volunteer for retraining programmes. Considerable anxiety may be attached to success in a new job which is only accentuated by the existing stereotype that the older person tends to be rigid and difficult to train. Given the choice of redundancy money or possible failure in retraining many seem to opt for the former. If training is chosen such anxiety may decrease the success of the programme. Even if training is successful Newsham (1969) demonstrated that there are 'critical periods of adjustment' lasting some weeks in which older trainees are more likely to leave.

The designer of any training programme, having identified all the likely sources of difficulty for the older trainee, is in a position to attempt to minimize them by adapting the programme to these special needs. The problem mentioned concerning the older trainee's attitudes is interesting since it emphasizes that the eventual effectiveness of any training programme on transfer to the job situation may ultimately depend more on the development of a good emotional adjustment or attitude rather than the acquisition of a new set of skills *per se*. Typically 'participation' in discussions is advocated to provide such adaptation.

Belbin (1964) describes well known studies in which training programmes were modified in an ongoing-fashion to suit the individual needs of the older trainee, with successful results. The training recommendations which emerged for the older trainee are presented in Table 7.1 from Newsham (1969).

Table 7.1 Problems of learning for the adult (Newsham, 1969)

Difficulties increase with age	Suggestions as to how the training could be suitably adapted for the older learner
1. When tasks involve the need for short-term memory	(a) Avoid verbal learning and the need for conscious memorising. This may often be accomplished by making use of 'cues' which guide the trainee.
	(b) When possible, use a method which involves learning a task as a whole. If it has to be learned in parts, these parts should be learned in cumulative stages (a, $a + b$, $a + b + c$, and so on).
	(c) Ensure consolidation of learning before passing on to the next task or to the next part of the same task (importance of self-testing and checking).
2. When there is 'interference' from other activities or from other learning	(a) Restrict the range of activities covered in the course.
	(b) Employ longer learning sessions than is customary for younger trainees (i.e. not necessarily a longer overall time, but longer periods without interruption).
	(c) To provide variety, change the method of teaching rather than the content of the course. A change of subject matter may lead to confusion between the subjects.

111

Table 7.1—continued

Difficulties increase with age	Suggestions as to how the training could be suitably adapted for the older learner
3. When there is need to translate information from one medium to another	(a) Avoid the use of visual aids which necessitate a change of logic or a change in the plan of presentation. (b) If simulators or training devices are to be used, then they must be designed to enable learning to be directly related to practice.
4. When learning is abstract or unrelated to realities	(a) Present new knowledge only as a solution to a problem which is already appreciated.
5. When there is need to 'unlearn' something for which the older learner has a predilection	(a) Ensure 'correct' learning in the first place. This can be accomplished by designing the training around tasks of graduated difficulty.
6. When tasks are 'paced'	(a) Allow the older learner to proceed at his own pace. (b) Allow him to structure his own programme within certain defined limits. (c) Aim at his beating his own targets rather than those of others.
7. As tasks become more complex	(a) Allow for learning by easy stages of increasing complexity.
8. When the trainee lacks confidence	(a) Use written instructions. (b) Avoid the use of production material too soon in the course. (c) Provide longer induction periods. Introduce the trainee very gradually both to new machinery and to new jobs. (d) Stagger the intake of trainees. (e) If possible, recruit groups of workmates. (f) Avoid formal tests. (g) Don't give formal time limits for the completion of the course.
9. When learning becomes mentally passive	(a) Use an open situation which admits discovery learning. (b) Employ meaningful material and tasks which are sufficiently challenging to an adult. (c) Avoid a blackboard and classroom situation or conditions in which trainees may in earlier years have experienced a sense of failure.

It is worthwhile examining how these recommendations were derived from a study of the problems of training letter sorters at the London Postal School. The task involved the trainee in being able to associate the names of streets with their correct postal district in the London area and subsequently sort letters into a 48-box frame involving these postal districts and categories such as 'foreign' and 'unpaid and underpaid'. The behavioural objective of the traditional training scheme was that the trainee was able to sort 500 incompletely addressed cards 'at the rate of thirty-three a minute with fewer than fifteen errors'. A greater percentage of trainees over forty were failing this criterion or required an extension to the training period.

The problems involved in training letter sorters were studied by the use of a pilot scheme, experimentation and observation and questioning of trainees. This led to an eventual modification of the traditional training programme along several dimensions. The modified training programme compared favourably with the traditional one although it is impossible to disentangle the relative effects of the many changes instituted and it is also difficult to interpret the increase in failure rate revealed by a follow-up study, although Belbin attributed the latter effect to shortcomings in training the instructors. Nevertheless Belbin's account is stimulating and intimates how some of the previously mentioned limitations of the older trainee may be manifested and overcome by training.

Some trainees performed adequately during training in heavily prompted situations (for example coloured card to same coloured box) but failed to learn the association between the address and postal district. Nevertheless prevention of early errors did seem important for the older trainee. Any prompting technique, used in the modified training programme, which had the desired effect of minimizing errors had to be evaluated against its possible inhibitory effect on real learning. In the traditional GPO training method prompts were provided on the back of sample letters indicating the correct postal district. However Belbin suggests that by the time the sorter had read the address, found the prompt on the back of the letter, located the correct box on the frame and posted it, the trainee 'would forget which place he was putting there'. Presumably this is due to a short-term memory limitation. These and other examples illustrated the limitation of the traditional training method and Belbin describes a programme to overcome them.

For example a progressive cumulative part training programme coupled with a longer period of practice would possibly reduce memory demands. These changes met with favourable reactions from the older trainees. Belbin's study of training letter sorters is therefore a classic example of how the trainer should attempt to match the programme to the individual needs of the older trainee.

Personality

Personality variables have not often been related to training. One would expect such traits as extraversion and introversion to be related particularly to the training of social skills or to the environment in which training takes place. Leith (1969) related the structure of programmed learning material to personality type. In a programme teaching Mendelian genetics extraverts were more successful with an unstructured and ambiguous programme whilst the reverse was true of introverts. Other studies have found that various personality pairings produce superior training results in programmed learning than solo performance. It is obvious that these isolated findings cannot provide guidelines for the trainer but at least they show the possibility of interaction between the trainee's personality and his general training environment.

In conclusion it seems that ideally the trainer should attempt to analyse the task demands and relate them and the design of the training programme to the trainee's ability and personality. Some crude indices of the trainee's ability can be gauged from his IQ and age which are associated with certain cognitive limitations. The effect of these will depend upon a certain number of factors although modest limitations can usually be circumvented by the use of carefully selected training methods.

8
Conclusions

In Chapters 1 and 3 the importance of viewing training in its context was stressed. The general model of skilled performance and associated training methods have principally been related to perceptual-motor skill learning. At this stage it is important to consider different contexts of training. The information processing model of skill should generally be useful in a variety of training situations, indicating task demands and drawing attention to learning difficulties. Also the training methods emphasize the importance of providing information concerning these task demands. The designer of the training programme must be aware of the advantages and disadvantages of any training method, in whatever context it is to be used.

In the complex diagram of the training system in Chapter 1 (Fig. 1.2), there are a number of regulators of the training design for any task. Consideration needs to be given to the location of training, materials and methods used, analysis of the task, the process of selection, the instructors or their substitutes and the organizational and social contexts of training. The training programme eventually produced may or may not be successful, which can be specified by a number of criteria.

Evaluation of training

The *Glossary of Training Terms* has defined evaluation as follows:

Evaluation. The assessment of the total value of a training system, training course or programme in social as well as financial terms. Evaluation differs from validation in that it attempts to measure the overall cost-benefit of the course or programme and not just the achievement of its laid down objectives. The term is also used in the general judgemental sense of the continuous monitoring of a programme or of the training function as a whole.

There are difficulties with this definition as Hamblin (1974) points out, because it is impossible to quantify what the social value will be, and even the financial gains and losses may be difficult to estimate. However obviously criteria exist for *validation* of a training programme, defined by the *Glossary* as:

Validation (of a training programme). 1. *Internal validation:* a series of tests and assessments designed to ascertain whether a training programme has achieved the behavioural objectives specified. 2. *External validation.* A series of tests and assessments designed to ascertain whether the behavioural objectives of an internally valid training programme were realistically based on an accurate initial identification of training needs in relation to the criteria of effectiveness adopted by the organization.

Hamblin criticizes this narrow definition, which excludes unanticipated effects, and prefers the broader definition, 'Any attempt to obtain information (feedback) on the effect of a training programme, and to assess the value of the training in the light of that information', which covers both evaluation and validation. There are various measures of the criteria for the evaluation of training. It is important to realize that evaluation should be an on-going process in order to ensure the continued effectiveness of the training over time and if circumstances change.

Internal validation illustrates that there is a close relationship between task analysis and evaluation. Task analysis is the first stage of the evaluation process because it specifies the behavioural objectives to be attained by the trainees. Thus a programmed text or a simulator will be evaluated in terms of the measurable learning outcomes they produce. Any training *method* used will of course generally have been evaluated by experimental research in different contexts as discussed in Chapters 4, 5 and 6. Its success under experimental scrutiny may indicate its potential for solving the training problem. For example, if the task consists of learning a long procedure of operations for assembling a machine component, the training system designer should consult the research literature in order to assess the possible effectiveness of part versus whole techniques.

In a system context, how effective is training in terms of the system demands and constraints? This refers to external validation of training which takes us a stage further than internal validation. Such evaluation views training in the wider context of the job and the overall system. An internally valid programme may be developed which may not be effective in the real job situation or may fail some system criterion such as cost effectiveness. An overall evaluation based on a combination of internal and external criteria is necessary but often very difficult. For example, a training programme may be devised which reduces training time dramatically, and appears highly cost effective. It may involve high investment in terms of equipment and materials, but reduce the drop-out rate of trainees, and also cut the cost of lack of production during training. Furthermore it may affect industrial relations, if the status and/or prospects of present job incumbents are threatened as a consequence. Therefore evaluation of training is performed at a number of levels and may have to use a range of methods. Hamblin (1974) gives five levels of effects of training which can be evaluated.

1. *Reactions*. This concerns the subjective evaluation of the training course by the trainees, in terms of their impressions, opinions and attitudes. Such reactions may be a function of the training content and methods used, its location, other trainees, the trainer, etc. The reactions will be there regardless of the trainer's intentions, and on some occasions may affect the attainment of the behavioural goals of the training programme. The trainer must therefore attempt to identify the reactions which may inhibit not only the internal but the external validation of the programme. Interview and questionnaire techniques are useful methods for collecting information about such reactions.

117

2. *Learning.* Training research has been mainly concerned with the evaluation of learning following different training methods. The learning/performance distinction was discussed in Chapter 2, emphasizing that learning can only be indirectly inferred from performance measurement. The main criteria for the selection of appropriate measures of performance must be their validity and reliability. That is, that they actually measure relevant dimensions of training and that their results are repeatable. Tests of training at this evaluation level have similar requirements to psychometric tests (see E2). Evaluation here is of the efficiency of the training programme rather than of the trainees, and any failure must be attributed to 'faults' in the training process. Davies (1972b) outlines four different tests which can be used in evaluation: (*a*) a 'prerequisites test' may be used either as a selection device determining whether the trainee will be able to cope with the training programme, or as an indication of whether any additional prior learning exercises are necessary; (*b*) a 'pre-test' can show parts of the training which may be omitted or the level of difficulties appropriate for the individual. It can also be used by the trainee to evaluate on-going performance through the programme; (*c*) a 'post-test' constitutes the usual evaluation of training, determining whether the objectives have been reached; (*d*) a 'retention' test measures performance some time after training and is similar to a post-test in that criterion performance is measured.

Retention of training has not been mentioned up to now, although it is particularly important where recently acquired skills are not practised and may be forgotten. The phenomenon of forgetting is well-documented for both verbal and perceptual-motor tasks (Adams, 1967). Some factors affecting retention are the nature of the task and how it is measured, the amount of training, the duration of the retention interval, and the nature and time of occurrence of any other activities performed before or after training.

Over brief periods of time up to one minute, retention of verbal material can deteriorate rapidly, particularly when rehearsal of the material is prevented in some way. Similarly some aspects of a motor response (e.g. movement extent or pressure) are also quickly forgotten although the reasons for this are probably very different compared with verbal short-term retention.

Continuous motor behaviour is classically viewed as very

resistant to forgetting over long periods of time. Driving is an example. The real argument here however is not so much empirical but which performance criterion to adopt. For example, driving may not be forgotten with a broad criterion of 'ability to drive without accident' which would be too insensitive to detect possible deterioration in clutch and gear control. A laboratory tracking study by Fleishman and Parker (1962) found that virtually no loss occurred until after fourteen months which was even then quickly relearned. Possibly the performance criterion was insensitive to miniscule changes in spatial and temporal accuracy. Noble and Trumbo (1967) have found a deterioration in these components over time, particularly timing accuracy which is consistent with beliefs that poor performance of ball sports after periods of no practice is principally due to a loss of 'timing'. Generally serial tasks involving a number of discrete responses are quickly forgotten (e.g. Neumann and Ammons, 1957) compared with the above-mentioned 'continuous' tasks.

3. *Job behaviour*. The training programme must not only be internally valid by achieving its behavioural objectives, but also externally valid with adequate job performance. The level of learning manifest in the job situation is determined by the amount of 'transfer of training', mentioned in Chapter 6. Measurement of transfer of training can be fairly straightforward for man-machine tasks, but may be more elusive in other jobs, e.g. those requiring social skills, such as customer service or supervisory training.

4. *Organization*. Hamblin (1974) suggests that training may also be evaluated in terms of changes in the functioning of the organization, for which Lindahl (1949) has presented eight criteria:

(*a*) quality of production
(*b*) number of operators able to reach job standards
(*c*) time required for a specific job
(*d*) damage to material or equipment
(*e*) absenteeism
(*f*) labour turnover
(*g*) running costs
(*h*) performance on personnel measures such as tests, rating scales and attitude surveys.

Hamblin further suggests that a fifth level may be distinguished although practically it will be closely associated with this one.

5. *Ultimate level*. Changes in job behaviour at the previous level are evaluated in terms of criteria of ultimate organizational goals, which are mainly financial. Whilst training can be evaluated in terms of cost effectiveness Hamblin (1974) states that,

> hospitals, schools, prisons, police forces, armies, welfare organizations, and even government departments may all give priority to some kind of measurement of *human good* over purely financial criteria, though the extent to which they are able to do this will depend on the amount of financial pressure placed on them at particular times. Even business organizations, which purport to exist solely in order to make a profit, may, in times of prosperity, carry out some activities (including training) which are not geared towards any financial goal, although they may still try to *rationalize* these activities in financial terms ... So the *hard-headed* view, which would automatically equate *ultimate value* with *costs* may in some cases be quite mistaken. (1974: 22)

Economic justifications for training are often forcefully argued, not least by those engaged in training research! Chaney and Teel (1967) mention a programme of research for improving inspection performance by training and the use of job aids which cost approximately $50,000 over two years, but yielded over $200,000 per year in documented cost savings.

Evaluation of training is a complex issue which may proceed at many levels. But the systems viewpoint outlined in Chapter 1 illustrates how evaluation is an essential feature of the organization of training. Efficient control of the system is only possible by the *feedback* which evaluation provides. The system can therefore not only correct its own errors but be adaptive to changing circumstances. Thus the same underlying principle of feedback control which is useful for describing human performance also provides a useful framework for describing the regulation of training systems.

Training and the future

This section covers some remaining issues in the area of training, which may be particularly pertinent in the future, and reviews the potential further use of the general model for training proposed in this book. The prediction of future trends in skill demands is particularly hazardous in our rapidly changing environment. However, the general model should be able to accommodate training of different skills with different demands since it emphasizes the functional components of training, rather than the specific activities involved. Nevertheless in the future the modes in which information may be transmitted in the tasks of the future may differ, and the trainer should therefore re-establish the optimal training method.

The future of skill

The model of skill developed from research into perceptual-motor skills. The understanding of such skills grew in the nineteen forties and fifties, and had immediate and obvious applications to the labour intensive manual skill based industry of that time (Seymour, 1954). Whilst such tasks are still important the orientation of industry has changed in many ways. A number of industries are now capital intensive, with automated plants, which are characterized by skills of a more problem-solving and decision-making nature. Such skills have been termed 'intellectual' or 'mental', thus emphasizing their central processing rather than motor aspects. An example would be the task of a process control operator, who monitors a display for changing process conditions and faults. If a fault occurs, it must be quickly identified and rectified by the controller. The skill lies in the interpretation of information from the display, and rapid diagnosis of the fault and selection of the appropriate course of action. All of these processes can be controlled by an overall 'plan' for fault finding and analysed in terms of the general feedback control model. Training provides the opportunity for learning the optimal plan, which has been isolated by task analysis. The diagnostic skills of process control are paralleled by those in electronics maintenance tasks. The growth in the use of electronic technology in industry and the home has resulted in a demand for people skilled in efficiently locating and rectifying faulty components.

A growth in service industries, e.g. hotel and catering, has emphasized the importance of skills of a different nature. The growth of this area has meant that people need training in social or interpersonal skills. Whilst this appears to be the domain of the social psychologist, Argyle (1967) has developed a model of interpersonal behaviour derived from a general model of perceptual-motor skill. He sees a close parallel between these two types of skill:

In the course of social interaction the participant responds to a series of noises and gestures on the part of another, by a series of noises and gestures and facial expressions of his own. The stimuli consist of the behaviour of others, and the responses involve mainly the voice and face, rather than the hands and feet.

It may be noted that serial motor skills consist of a very rapid series of motor responses in response to a rapidly changing situation – consider the speed of a pianist's reactions, for example. Social responses probably proceed at a similar pace. This is most clearly the case with speech and it will be shown that eye-movements are similarly paced. (1967: 86)

Argyle presents a social skill feedback model as shown in Fig. 8.1. This represents the situation from the perspective of one person, A, and of course another person, B, needs a similar model to represent his perspective of the situation.

The three feedback loops are:

X: Information about the success of A's social skill on B's behaviour,
Y: Information about the success of the interaction of A's and B's social techniques,
Z: Information that may change A's goals as a consequence of B's responses.

It can be seen that the same feedback control principles can be used here as in the perceptual-motor skill situation. The equilibrium system, in Fig. 8.1, refers to the synchronization of the social techniques of A and B during interaction and is controlled on the basis of both A and B striving to maintain a state of equilibrium.

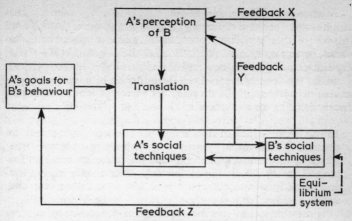

Fig. 8.1 *Social skill model (Argyle, 1967)*

As the skill model is useful for analysing these social skills, similar techniques of training can be applied and evaluated. Argyle outlines the different training methods for social skills. We have seen already that 'role-playing' can be viewed as a form of simulation, whilst a video-tape of such encounters can provide extrinsic terminal feedback. Concurrent feedback from the trainer via ear phones worn by the trainee can be delivered during role playing. A mirror may be used to provide the trainee with visual feedback of his own facial expression and is equivalent to concurrent extrinsic feedback. Such a device for training in role-playing situations can distract the trainee from the important intrinsic feedback from the other person. Tentatively this is consistent with the previously documented finding that concurrent feedback is often inappropriate for training.

The profile of skill demands required by industry is likely to move away from the perceptual-motor dimension. There may also be a growth in the importance of leisure and therefore 'recreational' skills. These may range from sports skills in which there are clear applications of traditional skill psychology (see Whiting, 1969) to a variety of 'bio-feedback' techniques aimed at developing control over biological states, some of which lead to increased relaxation. The present authors feel that the view of man as an information processor will be useful in all these different training situations.

Training populations

In a paper entitled *Training Entire Populations* by Conrad (1967), a special training problem of modern society is examined. Increasingly large proportions of the population are placed in situations in which new and rapid learning is necessary. This may be the consequence of the introduction of a new passenger transport system in which people may have to acquire such new skills as using an automated underground system or a one-man operated bus. Alternatively changes in communication systems such as more sophisticated telephones, postal codes and international road signs present new training problems. Other examples are the introduction of decimal currency and metrication and in the future the installation of computer voting systems. Such innovations may be beneficial to society in the long term but create considerable individual learning problems in the short term. The normal procedures for training are not possible in tackling these large scale learning problems. The trainee population is unselected, therefore including the complete range of individual differences. The communication between trainer and trainee is typically one way. Hence training proceeds in an 'open-loop' rather than a 'closed-loop' manner. Changes in behaviour are primarily effected by written instruction, mass media, etc. and the trainee will typically never receive extrinsic feedback. Such situations have been characterised by Lewis and Cook (1969) as 'telling' rather than 'teaching' ones; they point out that open-loop instruction may still be efficient if carefully designed.

The basic problem for instruction stems from ambiguities in language communication and also the difficulty of communicating logical rule structures to individuals in some linguistic form. Ambiguity in language may arise from grammatically correct sentences. For example Chapanis (1965) quoted the now famous example of a sign outside a lift in an American store, see Fig. 8.2.

There is obviously ambiguity in these instructions. Their purpose is to discourage people from using the lift, rather than to suggest they will get a better lift service by going to another floor. Other instructions may be simply difficult to process because of their linguistic form. For example, Jones (1968) found that when subjects are given the instructions, 'Mark all numbers except 2, 5, 8', they performed faster than when given 'Mark all the numbers but not 2, 5, 8'. Therefore presentation

```
PLEASE
WALK UP ONE FLOOR

WALK DOWN
TWO FLOORS

FOR IMPROVED
ELEVATOR SERVICE
```

Fig. 8.2 *Ambiguous instructions (After Chapanis, 1965)*

of instruction information must be as clear and unambiguous as possible. Research has demonstrated that algorithms are good methods for presenting complex (or even simple) logical sets of rules. In Table 8.1 is a typical piece of bureaucratic prose supposedly providing information about the new Capital Gains Tax of 1966. The algorithmic form of presentation in Fig. 8.3 is undoubtedly more comprehensible (Lewis *et al*, 1967). Thus if training is only possible on an open-loop basis the trainer must attempt to elicit immediate error-free performance.

Table 8.1 Extract from capital gains tax leaflet (Lewis *et al*, 1967)

(*i*) *If the asset consists of stocks or shares which have values quoted on a stock exchange (see also paragraph G below), or unit trust units whose values are regularly quoted, the gain or loss (subject to expenses) accruing after 6 April 1965, is the difference between the amount you received on disposal and the market value on 6 April 1965, except that in the case of a gain where the actual cost of the asset was higher than the value at 6 April 1965, the chargeable gain is the excess of the amount you received on disposal over the original cost or acquisition price; and in the case of a loss, where the actual cost of the asset was lower than the value at 6 April 1965, the allowable loss is the excess of the original cost or acquisition price over the amount received on disposal.*

If the substitution of original cost for the value at 6 April 1965, turns a gain into a loss, or a loss into a gain, there is, for the purposes of tax, no chargeable gain or allowable loss.

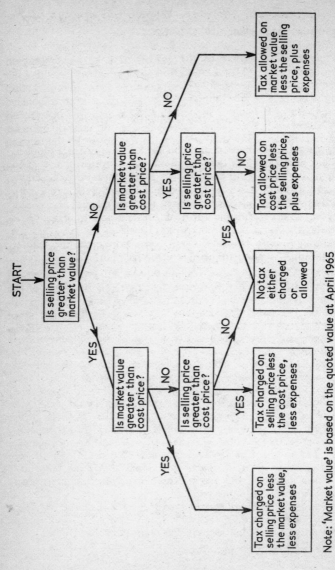

START

Is selling price greater than market value?

YES

Is market value greater than cost price?

NO

Is selling price greater than cost price?

YES

Tax charged on selling price less the cost price, less expenses

YES

Tax charged on selling price less the market value, less expenses

NO

No tax either charged or allowed

YES

Tax allowed on cost price less the selling price, plus expenses

NO

Is market value greater than cost price?

Is selling price greater than cost price?

NO

Tax allowed on market value less the selling price, plus expenses

Note: 'Market value' is based on the quoted value at April 1965

Fig. 8.3 Algorithm for capital gains tax (Lewis et al, 1967)

The future of training

In this book a picture of the contribution of psychology to training has been sketched and now we can briefly consider the directions for future research in training. The first direction should be in the development of better, more comprehensive taxonomies of behaviour for training. This area was introduced in Chapter 3, but as Miller (1967) points out such taxonomies still require more evaluation. Evaluation must be by testing how exhaustive and exclusive the taxonomic categories for training are by application to a range of tasks. The final criterion of a useful taxonomy is that the categories indicate the most appropriate training method to be used. This should also be the subject of further evaluation research. Research should continue into the efficiency of different training methods for a variety of tasks alongside inquiry into new methods and applications of theory. Ideally a technology of training would be based upon a matrix relating types of task to types of training method as outlined by Wallis *et al.* (1966). Each cell would contain details on the relevance and predicted efficiency of the training method under various conditions with different individuals. Progress towards this goal will be gradual, since human learning is a complex affair and past experience shows that we should not expect simple answers.

References and Name Index

The numbers in italics following each entry refer to page numbers within this book

Adams, J. A. (1967) *Human Memory*. New York: McGraw-Hill. *118*

Adams, J. A. (1968) Response feedback and learning. *Psychological Bulletin 70*: 486–504. *29, 31*

Adams, J. A. (1971) A closed-loop theory of motor learning. *Journal of Motor Behavior 3*: 111–49. *37, 38, 61, 65*

Adams, J. A. and Creamer, L. R. (1962) Anticipatory timing of continuous and discrete responses. *Journal of Experimental Psychology 63*: 84–90. *35*

Adams, J. A. and Hufford, L. E. (1962) Contributions of a part-task trainer to the learning and relearning of a time-shared flight manoeuvre. *Human Factors 4*: 159–70. *93*

Aiken, E. G. and Lau, A. W. (1967) Response prompting and response confirmation. A review of recent literature. *Psychological Bulletin 68*: 330–41. *70, 71*

Ammons, R. B. (1947) Acquisition of motor skill: II. Rotary pursuit performance with continuous practice before and after a single rest. *Journal of Experimental Psychology 37*: 393–411. *89*

Annett, J. (1959) Learning a pressure under conditions of immediate and delayed knowledge of results. *Quarterly Journal of Experimental Psychology 11*: 3–15. *32*

Annett, J. 1961) *The Role of Knowledge of Results in Learning: A Survey*. New York: U.S. Naval Training Devices Center. (Rep. no. 342–3). *31, 23*

Annett, J. (1966) Training for perceptual skills. *Ergonomics* 9: 459–68. *71*

Annett, J. (1968) A systems approach. In *Planning Industrial Training*. London: National Institute of Adult Education. *20, 21*

Annett, J. (1969) *Feedback and Human Behaviour*. Harmondsworth: Penguin. *26, 31, 61, 64*

Annett, J. (1970) The role of action feedback in the acquisition of simple motor responses. *Journal of Motor Behavior* 2: 217–21. *32*

Annett, J. and Duncan, K. D. (1967) Task analysis and training design. *Occupational Psychology* 41: 211–21. *48, 52, 54, 60*

Annett, J., Duncan, K. D., Stammers, R. B. and Gray, M. J. (1971) *Task Analysis*. Training Information No. 6, London: H.M.S.O. *46, 47, 52, 56, 57*

Annett, J. and Kay, H. (1956) Skilled performance. *Occupational Psychology* 30: 112–17. *86, 87*

Annett, J. and Paterson, L. (1967) Training for auditory detection. *Acta Psychologica* 27: 420–6. *72*

Argyle, M. (1967) *The Psychology of Interpersonal Behaviour*. Harmondsworth: Penguin. *122, 123*

Attneave, F. (1959) *Applications of Information Theory to Psychology*. New York: Holt, Rinehart and Winston. *26*

Belbin, E. (1964) *Training the adult worker*. (Problems of Progress in Industry No. 15.) London: H.M.S.O. *109, 111, 113*

Belbin, E. and Belbin, R. M. (1972) *Problems in Adult Retraining*. London: Heinemann. *109*

Belbin, E., Belbin, R. M. and Hill, F. (1957) A comparison between the results of three different methods of operator training. *Ergonomics* 1: 39–50. *71*

Biel, W. C. (1962) Training programs and devices. In R. M. Gagné (ed.) *Psychological Principles in System Development*. New York: Holt, Rinehart and Winston. *98, 100*

Bilodeau, E. A. and Bilodeau, I. McD. (1958) Variable frequency of knowledge of results and the learning of a simple skill. *Journal of Experimental Psychology* 55: 379–83. *65*

Bilodeau, I. McD. (1966). Information feedback. In E. A. Bilodeau (ed.) *Acquisition of Skill*. New York: Academic Press. *31, 64*

Birren, J. E. (1974) Translations in gerontology – from lab to life. Psychology and speed of response. *American Psychologist* 29: 808–15. *109*

Blum, M. L. and Naylor, J. C. (1968) *Industrial Psychology*. New York: Harper and Row. *60, 86*

Bramley, P. (1973) Equipment recognition training – learning wholes or individual features? *Occupational Psychology* 47: 131–9. *71*

Briggs G. E., Naylor, J. C. and Fuchs, A. H. (1962) *Whole versus part training as a function of task dimensions.* New York: U.S. Naval Training Devices Center (Rep. no. 950–2). *86*

Boucher, J. L. (1974) Higher processes in motor learning. *Journal of Motor Behavior* 6: 131–7. *37*

Carr, H. (1930) Teaching and learning. *Journal of Genetic Psychology* 31: 189–218. *68*

Chaney, F. B. and Teel, K. S. (1967) Improving inspector performance through training and visual aids. *Journal of Applied Psychology* 51: 311–15. *120*

Chapanis, A. (1959) *Research Techniques in Human Engineering.* Baltimore: Johns Hopkins Press. *60*

Chapanis, A. (1965) Words, words, words. *Human Factors* 7: 1–17. *124, 125*

Clarke, A. D. B. (1966) *Recent Advances in the Study of Subnormality.* London: National Association for Mental Health. *107*

Clarke, A. D. B. and Hermelin, B. F. (1955) Adult imbeciles: their abilities and trainability. *Lancet* 2: 337–9. *107*

Colquhoun, W. P. (1966) Training for vigilance: A comparison of different techniques. *Human Factors* 8: 7–12. *72*

Conrad, R. (1951) Study of skill by motion and time study and by psychological experiment. *Research* 4: 353–8. *48*

Conrad, R. (1967) Training entire populations. *Manpower and Applied Psychology* 1: 50–6. *124*

Cox, J. A., Wood, R. D., Jr. and Boren, L. M. (1965) *Functional and appearance fidelity of training devices for fixed procedures tasks.* Alexandria, Va: Human Resources Research Office. (Tech. Rep. no. 65) *99*

Crossman, E. R. F. W. (1956) Perceptual activities in manual work. *Research* 9: 42–9. *48*

Crossman, E. R. F. W. (1959) A theory of the acquisition of speed-skill. *Ergonomics* 2: 153–66. *36, 37, 85*

Crossman, E. R. F. W. (1960). *Automation and Skill.* (D.S.I.R. Problems of Progress in Industry, No. 9.) London: M.M.S.O. *14*

Crossman, E. R. F. W. (1964) Information processes in human skill. *British Medical Bulletin* 20: 32–7. *27*

Crossman, E. R. F. W. and Szafran, J. (1956) Changes with age in the speed of information intake and discrimination. *Experi-*

mentia Supplement 4: 128–35. *109*

Crowder, N. A. (1960) Automatic tutoring by intrinsic programming. In A. A. Lunsdaine and R. Glaser (eds) *Teaching Machines and Programmed Learning*. Washington: N.E.A. *78*

Dale, H. C. A. (1958) Fault-finding in electronic equipment. *Ergonomics 1*: 356–85. *108*

Davies, I. K. (1972a) Presentation strategies. In J. Hartley (ed.) *Strategies for Programmed Instruction: An Educational Technology*. London: Butterworths. *77*

Davies, I. K. (1972b) *The Management of Learning*. London: McGraw-Hill. *118*

Davies, J. P. (1972) *Task analysis and an approach to coaching in sport*. Unpublished M.Sc. Dissertation, Applied Psychology Dept., University of Aston in Birmingham. *57, 58*

Department of Employment (1971) *Glossary of Training Terms* (2nd edn). London: H.M.S.O. *10, 11, 46, 96, 115, 116*

Duncan, K. D. (1969) Task analysis evaluated. In A. de Brisson (ed.) *Programmed Learning Research: Major Trends*. Paris: Dunod. *81*

Duncan, K. D. (1971) Long-term retention and transfer of an industrial search skill. *British Journal of Psychology 62*: 439–48. *108*

Duncan, K. D. (1972) Strategies for analysis of the task. In J. Hartley (ed.) *Strategies for Programmed Instruction: An Educational Technology*. London: Butterworths. *57, 59, 60, 81*

Dyal, J. A. (1966) Effects of delay of knowledge of results and subject response bias on extinction of a simple motor skill. *Journal of Experimental Psychology 71*: 559–63. *64*

Eckstrand, G. A. (1964) *Current status of the technology of training*. Wright-Patterson A. F. B. Aerospace Medical Labs., Rep. AMRL – TDR – 64–86. *19*

Edwards, E. (1964) *Information Transmission*. London: Chapman and Hall. *26, 28*

Ellis, H. C. (1965) *The Transfer of Learning*. New York: Macmillan. *96, 97*

Ferguson, G. A. (1954) On learning and human ability. *Canadian Journal of Psychology 8*: 95–112. *102*

Fitts, P. M. (1951) Engineering psychology and equipment design. In S. S. Stevens (ed.) *Handbook of Experimental Psychology*. New York: Wiley. *25, 106*

Fitts, P. M. (1954) The information capacity of the human motor system in controlling the amplitude of movement. *Journal of Experimental Psychology 47*: 381–91. *30*

Fitts, P. M. (1962) Factors in complex skill training. In R. Glaser (ed.) *Training Research and Education*. University of Pittsburgh. (Reprinted 1965 New York: Wiley). *38, 39, 106*

Fitts, P. M. and Peterson, J. R. (1964) Information capacity of discrete motor responses. *Journal of Experimental Psychology* 67: 103–12. *30*

Fitts, P. M. and Posner, M. I. (1967) *Human Performance*. Belmont, California: Brooks-Cole. *11, 26, 27, 42*

Flanagan, J. C. (1954) The critical incident technique. *Psychological Bulletin* 51: 327–58. *60*

Fleishman, E. A. (1966) Human abilities and the acquisition of skill. Comments on Professor Jones's paper. In E. A. Bilodeau (ed.) *Acquisition of Skill*. New York: Academic Press. *103*

Fleishman, E. A. (1968) Individual differences and motor learning. In R. M. Gagné (ed.) *Learning and Individual Differences*. Columbus: Merrill Books. *106*

Fleishman, E. A. and Fruchter, B. (1960) Factor structure and predictability of successive stages of learning Morse Code. *Journal of Applied Psychology* 44: 97–101. *106*

Fleishman, E. A. and Hempel, W. E., Jr. (1955) The relation between abilities and improvement with practice in a visual discrimination reaction task. *Journal of Experimental Psychology* 49: 301–12. *104*

Fleishman, E. A. and Parker, J. F. (1962) Factors in the retention and relearning of perceptual-motor skill. *Journal of Experimental Psychology* 64: 215–26. *119*

Fleishman, E. A. and Rich, S. (1963) Role of kinesthetic and spatial-visual abilities in perceptual-motor learning. *Journal of Experimental Psychology* 66: 6–11. *104, 105*

Fox, P. W. and Levy, C. M. (1969) Acquisition of a simple motor response as influenced by the presence or absence of action visual feedback. *Journal of Motor Behavior* 1: 169–80. *66*

Fuchs, A. H. (1962) The progression–regression hypotheses in perceptual-motor skill learning. *Journal of Experimental Psychology* 63: 177–82. *36*

Furneaux, W. D. (1960) Intellectual abilities and problem-solving behaviour. In H. J. Eysenck (ed.) *Handbook of Abnormal Psychology*. London: Pitman. *107*

Gagné, R. M. (1962a) Military training and principles of learning. *American Psychologist* 17: 83–91. *14*

Gagné, R. M. (1962b) Simulators. In R. Glaser (ed.) *Training Research and Education*. University of Pittsburgh Press. (Reprinted, 1965, New York: Wiley). *91, 94*

Gagné, R. M. (1965) The analysis of instructional objectives for the design of instruction. In R. Glaser (ed.) *Teaching Machines and Programmed Learning*, 2. Washington: N.E.A. *81*

Gagné, R. M. (1970) *The Conditions of Learning* (2nd edn). New York: Holt, Rinehart and Winston. *50, 51, 80, 81*

Gibbs, C. B. (1954) The continuous regulation of skilled response by kinaesthetic feedback. *British Journal of Psychology 45*: 24–39. *34*

Glaser, R. (1962) Psychology and instructional technology. In R. Glaser (ed.) *Training Research and Education*. University of Pittsburgh. (Reprinted 1965, New York: Wiley). *12*

Greenspoon, J. and Foreman, S. (1956) Effect of delay of knowledge of results on learning a motor task. *Journal of Experimental Psychology 51*: 226–8. *64*

Gropper, G. L. (1968) Programmed visual presentations for procedural learning. *Audio-Visual Communication Review 16*: 33–5. *107*

Hamblin, A. C. (1974) *Evaluation and Control and Training*. London: McGraw-Hill. *116, 117, 119, 120*

Hammerton, M. (1966) Factors affecting the use of simulators for training. *Proc. I.E.E. 113*: 1881–4. *99*

Hammerton, M. (1967) Measures for the efficiency of simulators as training devices. *Ergonomics 10*: 63–5. *98*

Hartley, J. (1972a) Evaluation. In J. Hartley (ed.) *Strategies for Programmed Instruction: An Educational Technology*. London: Butterworths. *79, 80*

Hartley, J. (1972b) (ed.) *Strategies for Programmed Instruction: An Educational Technology*. London: Butterworths. *74, 75*

Henry, J. P. (1973) *An experimental evaluation of a shadowgraph simulator for driver training*. Crowthorne, Berks: Transport and Road Research Lab., Rep. LR 540. *94, 95*

Hick, W. E. (1952) On the rate of gain of information. *Quarterly Journal of Experimental Psychology 4*: 11–26. *30*

Hilgard, E. R. and Bower, G. H. (1966) *Theories of Learning* (3rd edn). New York: Appleton-Century-Crofts. *22, 23, 24*

Hill, W. F. (1972) *Learning* (2nd edn). London: University Paperbacks. *22*

Holding, D. H. (1965) *Principles of Training*. Oxford: Pergamon. *11, 62, 68, 89, 96*

Holding, D. H. (1970) Repeated errors in motor learning. *Ergonomics 13*: 727–34. *67*

Holding, D. H. and Macrae, A. W. (1964) Guidance, restriction and knowledge of results. *Ergonomics 7*: 289–95. *68*

Holding, D. H. and Macrae, A. W. (1966) Rate and force of guidance in perceptual-motor tasks with reversed or random spatial correspondence. *Ergonomics 9*: 289–96. *69*

Holloway, C. (1974) Organization, feedback and goal-directed behaviour. In *Human Information Processing* (Part 1). Open University Press. *40*

Jamieson, G. H. (1973) Simulation: Some implications of skill learning theory. *Programmed Learning and Educational Technology 10*: 239–47. *99*

Johnson, W. L. (1968) Flight simulation and airline pilot training. In J. M. Rolfe (ed.) *Vehicle Simulation for Training and Research*. Farnborough: R.A.F. Institute of Aviation Medicine, Rep. no. R.442. *92, 93*

Jones, S. (1968) Instructions, self-instructions and performance. *Quarterly Journal of Experimental Psychology 20*: 74–8. *124*

Kay, H., Annett, J. and Sime, M. E. (1963) *Teaching machines and their use in industry*. (Problems of Progress in Industry, No. 14.) London: H.M.S.O. *75*

Kay, H., Dodd, B. and Sime, M. (1968) *Teaching Machines and Programmed Instruction*. Harmondsworth: Penguin. *74*

Keele, S. W. (1968) Movement control in skilled motor performance. *Psychological Bulletin 70*: 387–403. *34, 39*

Keele, S. W. and Posner, M. I. (1968) Processing of visual feedback in rapid movements. *Journal of Experimental Psychology 77*: 155–8. *35*

Kimble, G. A. (1961) *Hilgard and Marquis's Conditioning and Learning* (2nd edn). New York: Appleton-Century-Crofts. *24*

Lashley, K. S. (1917) The accuracy of movement in the absence of excitation from the moving organ. *American Journal of Physiology 43*: 169–94. *34*

Laszlo, J. I. (1967) Training of fast tapping with reduction of kinaesthetic, tactile, visual and auditory sensations. *Quarterly Journal of Experimental Psychology 19*: 344–9. *34*

Lawson, T. E. (April 1974) Gagnés learning theory applied to technical instruction. *Training and Development Journal*, 32–40. *83*

Lee, B. S. (1951) Artificial stutter. *Journal of Speech and Hearing Disorders 16*: 53–5. *33*

Leith, G. O. M. (1969) Personality and learning. In W. R. Dunn and C. Holroyd (eds) *Aspects of Educational Technology*, II. London: Methuen. *114*

Leplat, J. and Bisseret, A. (1966) Analysis of the processes involved in the treatment of information by the air traffic controller. *The Controller 5*: 13–22. *60*

Lewis, B. N. and Cook, J. A. (1969) Toward a theory of telling.

International Journal of Man-Machine Studies 1: 129–76. *124*

Lewis, B. N., Horabin, I. S. and Gane, C. D. (1967) *Flow Charts, Logical Trees and Algorithms for Rules and Regulations.* CAS Occasional Paper No. 2. London: H.M.S.O. *17, 125, 126*

Lindahl, L. G. (1949) How to build a training program. *Personnel Journal* 27: 417–19. *119*

Lumsdaine, A. A. (1962) Experimental research on instructional devices and materials. In R. Glaser (ed.) *Training Research and Education.* University of Pittsburgh. (Reprinted, 1965, New York: Wiley.) *100*

Macrae, A. W. and Holding, D. H. (1965a) Method and task in motor guidance. *Ergonomics* 8: 315–20. *69*

Macrae, A. W. and Holding, D. H. (1965b) Guided practice in direct and reversed serial tracking. *Ergonomics* 8: 487–92. *69*

Macrae, A. W. and Holding, D. H. (1966) Transfer of training after guidance or practice. *Quarterly Journal of Experimental Psychology* 18: 327–33. *69*

McGuigan, F. J. (1959) The effect of precision, delay, and schedule of knowledge of results on performance. *Journal of Experimental Psychology* 58: 79–84. *64*

Mager, R. F. (1961) *Preparing Instructional Objectives.* Palo Alto: Fearon Publishers. *12*

Miller, G. A., Galanter, E. and Pribram, K. H. (1960) *Plans and the Structure of Behavior.* New York: Holt, Rinehart and Winston. *40, 41, 52*

Miller, R. B. (1953) *Handbook on training and training equipment design.* Wright-Patterson A. F. B.: Wright Air Development Center, Rep. No. 53–136. *32*

Miller, R. B. (1954) *Psychological considerations in the design of training equipment.* Wright-Patterson A. F. B.: Wright Air Development Center, Rep. No. 54–563. *97, 98*

Miller, R. B. (1967) Task taxonomy: science or technology? *Ergonomics* 10: 167–76. *48, 50, 127*

Moray, N. (1967) Where is capacity limited? A survey and a model. *Acta Psychologica* 27: 84–92. *30*

Murrell, K. F. H. (1962) Industrial aspects of ageing. *Ergonomics* 5: 147–53. *109*

Naylor, J. C. (1962) *Parameters affecting the relative effectiveness of part and whole training methods: A review of the literature.* New York: U.S. Naval Training Devices Center Rep. No. 950–1. *85*

Naylor, J. C. and Briggs, G. E. (1963) Effects of task complexity and task organization on the relative efficiency of part and whole training methods. *Journal of Experimental Psychology* 65: 217–24. *85, 86*

Neumann, E. and Ammons, R. B. (1957) Acquisition and long-term retention of a simple serial perceptual-motor skill. *Journal of Experimental Psychology* 53: 159–61. *119*

Newsham, D. B. (1969) *The Challenge of Change to the Adult Trainee*. Training Information, Paper 3. London: H.M.S.O. *109, 110, 111, 112*

Nixon, K. (1974) Customer contact skills. *Industrial and Commercial Training* 8: 24–30. *95*

Noble, M. and Trumbo, D. (1967) The organization of skilled response. *Organizational Behavior and Human Performance* 2: 1–25. *119*

Pew, R. W. (1966) Acquisition of hierarchical control over the temporal organization of a skill. *Journal of Experimental Psychology* 71: 764–71. *43*

Postman, L. (1947) The history and present status of the law of effect. *Psychological Bulletin* 44: 489–563. *24*

Prather, D. C. (1973) Prompted mental practice as a flight simulator. *Journal of Applied Psychology* 57: 353–5. *96*

Prather, D. C. and Berry, G. A. (1970) Comparison of trial-and-error versus highly prompted learning of a perceptual skill. *Proceedings of the 78th Annual Convention of the A.P.A.* *72*

Rabbitt, P. M. A. (1965) An age decrement in the ability to ignore irrelevant information. *Journal of Gerontology* 20: 233–8. *109*

Robb, M. D. (1972) *The Dynamics of Motor-Skill Acquisition*. Englewood Cliffs, N.J.: Prentice-Hall. *66*

Rogers, C. A. (1974) Feedback precision and post feedback interval duration. *Journal of Experimental Psychology* 102: 604–8. *64*

Schori, T. R. (1970) Driving simulation: An overview. *Behavioral Research and Highway Safety* 1: 236–48. *94*

Seymour, W. D. (1954) *Industrial Training for Manual Operations*. London: Pitman. *121*

Seymour, W. D. (1966) *Industrial Skills*. London: Pitman. *47, 85*

Scott, M. G. (1955) Measurement of kinesthesis. *Research Quarterly* 26: 324–41. *29*

Sheffield, F. D. (1961) Theoretical considerations in the learning of complex sequential tasks from demonstration and practice. In A. A. Lumsdaine (ed.) *Student Response in Programmed Instruction*. Washington: NAS-NRC, Publication No. 943. *87*

Shannon, C. E. (1948) A mathematical theory of communication. *Bell System Technical Journal* 27 : 379–423, 623–56. *25, 26*

Singleton, W. T. (1968) Some recent experiments on learning and their training implications. *Ergonomics 11* : 53–9. *46*

Skinner, B. F. (1953) *Science and Human Behaviour.* New York Macmillan. *24*

Skinner, B. F. (1954) The science of learning and the art of teaching. *Harvard Educational Review 24* : 86–97. *77*

Sleeman, D. H. and Hartley, J. R. (1969) Instructional models in a computer-based learning system. *International Journal of Man-Machine Studies 1* : 177–88. *79*

Smith, K. U. (1966) Cybernetic theory and analysis of learning. In E. A. Bilodeau (ed.) *Acquisition of Skill.* New York : Academic Press. *33*

Smoll, F. L. (1971) Effects of precision of information feedback upon the acquisition of a motor skill. *Research Quarterly 43* : 489–93. *64*

Spence, K. W. (1951) Theoretical interpretations of learning. In S. S. Stevens (ed.) *Handbook of Experimental Psychology.* New York : Wiley. *23*

Stolurow, L. M. (1967) A computer assisted instructional system in theory and research. In *Aspects of Educational Technology.* London : Methuen *79*

Stratton, G. M. (1896) Some preliminary experiments in vision without inversion of the retinal image. *Psychological Review 3* : 611–17. *33*

Sulzer, J. L. and Levy, C. M. (1966). Goal and error training methods in the learning of a positioning response. *Psychonomic Science 6* : 179–80. *69*

Talland, G. A. (1968) Age and span of immediate recall. In G. A. Talland (ed.) *Human Ageing and Behavior.* New York : Academic Press. *109, 110*

Thorndike, E. L. (1913) *The Psychology of Learning.* New York : Teachers College. *24*

Thorndike, E. L. (1927) The law of effect. *American Journal of Psychology 39* : 212–22. *63*

Toye, M. (1969) A rethink on basic skills. *Industrial Training International 4* : 112–19. *85, 95*

Trowbridge, M. H. and Cason, H. (1932) An experimental study of Thorndike's theory of learning. *Journal of Genetic Psychology 7* : 245–60. *63*

Victor, J. E. (1971) What's wrong with analytic training? *The Bobbin 12* : 40–52. *85*

Wallis, D. (1966) The technology of military training. In W. M.

Jessop (ed.) *Manpower Planning*. New York: American Elsevier. *14*

Wallis, D., Duncan, K. D. and Knight, M. A. G. (1966) *Programmed Instruction in the British Armed Forces*. London: H.M.S.O. *77, 127*

Weisz, A. Z. and McElroy, L. S. (1964) *Response and feedback techniques for automated training of visual identification skills*. New York: U.S. Naval Training Devices Center, Rep. 789–3. *73*

Welford, A. T. (1958) *Ageing and Human Skill*. Oxford University Press for the Nuffield Foundation. *109*

Welford, A. T. (1968) *Fundamentals of Skill*. London: Methuen. *28, 29, 65, 89, 90*

Whiting, H. T. A. (1969) *Acquiring Ball Skill: A Psychological Interpretation*. London: Bell. *123*

Wiener, E. L. and Attwood, D. A. (1968) Training for vigilance: Combined cueing and knowledge of results. *Journal of Applied Psychology 52*: 474–9. *72*

Wiener, N. (1948) *Cybernetics*. New York: Wiley. *25, 34*

von Wright, J. M. (1957) A note on the role of guidance in learning. *British Journal of Psychology. 48*: 133–7. *68*

Wulff, J. J. and Berry, P. C. (1966) Aids to job performance. In R. M. Gagné (ed.) *Psychological Principles in System Development*. New York: Holt, Rinehart and Winston. *59*

Subject Index

142

143